D0504949

101
THINGS TO
DO BEFORE
YOU'RE FIVE

By the same author

The Girls' Book of Glamour: A Guide to being a Goddess
The Girls' Book 2: How to be the Best at Everything Again

101 THINGS TO DO BEFORE YOU'RE FIVE

The funny, bizarre and downright yucky things to expect from your little people

SALLY NORTON

VIKING
an imprint of
PENGUIN BOOKS

VIKING

Published by the Penguin Group

Penguin Books Ltd, 80 Strand, London WC2R 0RL, England

Penguin Group (USA) Inc., 375 Hudson Street, New York, New York 10014, USA

Penguin Group (Canada), 90 Eglinton Avenue East, Suite 700, Toronto, Ontario,
Canada M4P 2Y3 (a division of Pearson Penguin Canada Inc.)

Penguin Ireland, 25 St Stephen's Green, Dublin 2, Ireland
(a division of Penguin Books Ltd)

Penguin Group (Australia), 250 Camberwell Road, Camberwell, Victoria 3124,
Australia (a division of Pearson Australia Group Pty Ltd)

Penguin Books India Pvt Ltd, 11 Community Centre, Panchsheel Park,
New Delhi – 110 017, India

Penguin Group (NZ), 67 Apollo Drive, Rosedale, North Shore 0632,
New Zealand (a division of Pearson New Zealand Ltd)

Penguin Books (South Africa) (Pty) Ltd, 24 Sturdee Avenue,
Rosebank, Johannesburg 2196, South Africa

Penguin Books Ltd, Registered Offices: 80 Strand,
London WC2R 0RL, England

www.penguin.com

First published 2010

1

Copyright © Sally Norton, 2010

Illustration Copyright © Joe Berger, 2010

The moral right of the author has been asserted

Set in Aunt Mildred, Acro crayon and Superior regular

Printed in Great Britain by Clays Ltd, St Ives plc

A CIP catalogue record for this book is available from the British Library

ISBN: 978-0-670-91794-5

For George and Kate,
And in memory of my lovely dad, Ray Norton

ACKNOWLEDGEMENTS

A hundred and one thanks are due to my fantastic agent Jane Villiers and the crack team at Sayle Screen for all their advice and support; to Venetia Butterfield at Viking for showing such enthusiasm for this book from the very start; to Joe Berger for his wonderful illustrations; and to the brilliant, hard-working team at Penguin, especially Ellie Smith, Sarah Fraser and Kate Brotherhood.

Finally I'd like to thank 'our Kate' and all her fantastic friends who have provided the inspiration for this book – in particular, Joe and Nate, Felix and Bobby, Anna and Lucy B, Lucy P and Billy, Genevieve and Gene, Martha and Noah, Ben and Beth, Ruby, Isabel, Maia and Nicholas.

INTRODUCTION

Congratulations, you've been born! But don't just lie there gurgling. You've got lots to do before you turn five and are packed off to school. In fact, you've got 101 things to do.

You're only little now, but in the blink of an eye you'll be walking through the gates of academia. You'll be someone who has redefined the word 'holiday' for their parents, and a highly evolved human being who can win an argument simply by using three words – 'no', 'no' and 'no'.

Sometimes you'll find the journey from cradle to reception class frightening or just plain confusing. But don't fret – lots of people worry about being washed down the plughole with the dirty bathwater, and you won't be the first child to tip a bowl of cereal over your own head.

Other days you'll take things in your stride. You'll create finger paintings so good your parents will consider selling them on eBay as pictures 'in the style of Jackson Pollock', or demonstrate such silky football skills they'll become convinced they've got the next David Beckham on their hands.

Only one thing's guaranteed – that the time will pass quicker than anyone could anticipate and suddenly you'll be five years old. So, treasure this time. Roll down every hill you can, jump in every puddle whether you're wearing wellies or not, and always wipe that snotty nose on mummy's skirt. Because soon the fun and frolics of the first five years will be behind you, and you'll be facing a whole new set of adventures at Big School.

Seize the day, live life to the max and have fun while you can!

AGED 0-1 YEARS

THE EARLY DAYS OF BABYDOM

You'll start your first year unable either to support the weight of your own head or to tell the difference between daddy and a hat stand. But that's no excuse for just lazing around blowing milky bubbles. If you don't get on with things, you'll suddenly find you're one year old and full of regret for what might have been.

It's hard to believe now as you drool over mummy's shoulder, but one day you'll be grown up with your own job – maybe you'll be a teacher, a doctor, or a High Court judge that sends people to prison. Perhaps you'll even turn out to be a pop star, a footballer or the Dalai Lama!

Achieving some key goals now will really set you on the road to success – but remember, you've only got twelve months. Don't rely on mummy and daddy for help. If you're their first child, they'll be too terrified to trim your toenails at this stage, never mind showing you how to roll from the bathmat to the tiny space behind the loo as an adult is reaching for a clean nappy; and if they're old hands at the parenting lark, they'll be too busy stopping their big children destroying the house to show you how to do the loudest windy pop in the world.

So, come on, you've got to get through twelve clean Baby-gros a day, regurgitate at least a dozen feeds a week and make an attempt to cut a couple of teeth. If you've got the courage, you can achieve it all before you blow out the candle on your first birthday cake. Good luck!

 # GET WOKEN UP BY MUMMY CHECKING YOU'RE STILL ALIVE

There you are . . . in the Land of Nod . . . dreaming that you're drifting along on a river of milk, and watching the clouds and smiley faces float overhead, when suddenly you get the sensation of cold glass at the end of your nose. You open your eyes to find mummy leaning over your cot, a worried look on her face as she holds a small mirror under your nostrils.

It's a weird fact that the very same parents who spend hours on complicated bedtime routines to ensure you sleep soundly also persist in waking you up seven times a night to check you're still breathing. And as if that wasn't bad enough, they then want you to go straight back to sleep, so they can watch the second half of *CSI: Miami*.

LOOK JUST LIKE DADDY

Don't worry. Most babies look like their daddy for a while after they're born . . . and it's not just the side parting and football shirt that does it.

In the early days, you'll notice that everyone makes a point of saying that you've got your father's eyes, your father's nose, or maybe it's just the way you're 'always holding a bottle'. The evolutionary reason for this is to ensure the father believes the child is his and doesn't kill it. These days it's to ensure the father believes the child is his and keeps putting the bins out.

This is fine if you're a boy but it can be a bit embarrassing if you're a girl and daddy's a prop for the England rugby team. If this is the case, you've just got to hang on in there through the chunky phase until you start looking more like mummy.

Note: if mummy's a prop for the England women's rugby team, then you're really stuffed.

3 SCARE AN UNCLE WITH THE PULSE IN YOUR HEAD

After you've been photographed with your proud-but-terrified uncle, he'll be left to cuddle you for a few awkward moments while daddy gives a graphic description of the birth to the other family members present. If your uncle hasn't had kids yet, this is the perfect opportunity to scare him out of his wits.

The first thing he'll notice is the pulse beating in the soft part of your skull. No one will have bothered to tell him that the bones in your head haven't fully joined yet, that this gap is called the 'fontanelle', and that it's completely normal – he'll think an alien is about to burst out of your brain. Now look at him in a funny way – your newborn squint comes in very handy here. You can really unsettle him by keeping one beady eye on him and the other on the telly.

As you sense his arm going to sleep underneath you, do your final trick. Just work a hand free from the swaddling blanket and give yourself a quick wallop round the chops. Start crying hysterically, while looking accusingly at your uncle. He'll hold you like you're a bomb that's about to explode ... till mummy comes to rescue you.

Following this incident, you'll have very little to do with your uncle until mummy forces him to babysit one night when she has run out of other options.

4 TAKE AN IRRATIONAL DISLIKE TO A FAMILY MEMBER

You have so many visitors after you're born that it's hard to tell one from another. Some of them seem really lovely, but it's best not to develop favourites until you work out who's highest in the family pecking order – such as grandparents and others likely to provide expensive gifts or babysitting services.

But one thing's for sure – you're not going to like them all. It's hard to pinpoint exactly what it is about some people – perhaps it's their spotty face, or maybe it's the fact that you didn't hear them enter the room, then suddenly noticed them just standing there with their big black coat and big black beard.

Don't waste time trying to work out what you don't like about them. Even if mummy and daddy say, 'Don't be frightened of Uncle Michael, darling. He's going to be your godfather' ...

JUST SCREAM THE PLACE DOWN!

Mummy may try to calm you down by handing you over to Uncle Michael. Carry on screaming until he hands you back.

Mummy will try to reassure Uncle Michael that you like him really, and you are just tired and hungry. But when he leaves they'll wonder whether there is something wrong with him – perhaps babies are like dogs and instinctively know when someone's evil? Perhaps you do.

5 SLEEP LIKE A BABY – STAY UP ALL NIGHT

Lull your parents into a false sense of security in the first three days after you're born by sleeping soundly 99 per cent of the time. Mummy and daddy will be so thrilled you're already 'sleeping through' they'll stay up late watching movies and eating crisps. They'll ignore people's advice to 'sleep when the baby's sleeping' because, clearly, you're a very, very easy baby.

Once the friends have drifted away and granny's gone home, safe in the knowledge she's not needed, it's time to wake up. And stay awake.

It'll now take you around six months to work out the difference between night and day. But don't worry, because there's loads you can do. Why not stay up all night . . .

* Crying because you're hungry?
* Crying because you've got wind?
* Crying because you don't want to be picked up?
* Crying because you want to be picked up?
* Crying because you're tired?

Gradually you'll start to recognize your bedtime routine. The blinds will be down in your bedroom, twinkly music will be playing and mummy will be saying to daddy, 'Will you please stop blowing raspberries on the baby's tummy . . . it's waking him up.'

6 GET MUMMY TO GHOSTWRITE YOUR THANK-YOU LETTERS

Grown-ups expect thank-you letters for gifts they've sent you, even though you're not old enough to hold a pen without stabbing yourself in the eye. Manners are important – if you don't send auntie a thank-you letter pronto, she'll never give you a present again, or she'll give you clothes. The best way round this is to employ mummy as your ghostwriter. Here's what she needs to do:

1. Address the recipient by name, thank them for the gift and make some friendly comment: 'Dear Auntie Karen, thank you for the plastic rattle you sent me. I loved the bite marks on the handle . . . it's so nice to know I'm not the only baby who's played with it.'

2. Write how you plan to use the gift: 'I intend to shake it and chew on the handle.'

3. Always include at least three exclamation marks!!!

4. Add a line to update the giver about yourself: 'I've enjoyed my first three days of life and hope to start recognizing family members soon.'

5. Finish with an enquiry about their life: 'I hope you're enjoying work in the charity shop and are not drinking as much as usual.'

Top tip: *get mummy to enclose a photograph of you holding the present. After all, mummy's got a lot of time on her hands at the moment – you're nearly always asleep.*

x x x

7 PRESERVE YOUR FOOT-PRINTS FOR POSTERITY

Millions of parents have the brilliantly original idea of taking an imprint of their newborn's feet. They then frame it and either hang it up in the front room or give it to granny for Christmas.

If your parents didn't bother to pack a baby-footprint kit in the hospital bag, they had better get on with it, because your feet are getting bigger every day, and small feet are definitely the cutest.

Imagine what fun it'll be comparing your huge adult feet with your tiny baby prints – always a winner at an eighteenth birthday party. These are your options:

* Clay is the deluxe option because it feels so nice and squishy between your toes. Tricky to wash off, though, and you'll find dried bits of it in your socks for weeks.
* Ink will do at a pinch, though mummy will probably worry about whether it's organic, and if it'll harm your delicate skin.

And take your time. Did Leonardo dash off the *Mona Lisa* in ten minutes at the print shop? No. He was an artist, and so are you. In fact, what you're doing is harder, because you're using your feet. Have as many attempts as you feel you need even if it takes all the clay and ink in the shop, they're your feet and they're worth getting right – even if does end up costing mummy and daddy three times as much.

8 SLEEP WITH YOUR EYES OPEN

You get a lot of presents in the early days, and the best way to ensure no one nicks them is to sleep with your eyes open. Okay, so people say you should be able to trust your parents, but, honestly, how long have you actually known them? It's best to be alert to anything dodgy going on around you until you're really settled in.

Note: sleeping with your eyes open is a skill that will soon be lost. In fact, the only adults who have learned to do it are found in prisons – so enjoy it while you can.

Don't forget to experiment. Why not sleep with just one eye open, like a spy? Or go for the full horror effect by rolling your eyes back into your head so just the whites are showing?

 # SMILE YOUR FIRST GUMMY SMILE

You'll probably be photographed hundreds of times in the first few weeks. These are some of the photographs that will be taken:

* You and mummy in hospital (doesn't she look tired?).
* You in a plastic crib with daddy peering in.
* You in a blanket marked 'property of Homerton Hospital, Hackney' (daddy forgot to pack the hand-made, organic cotton receiving blanket mummy bought for fifty quid when she was very hormonal).
* You and granddad.
* You on granny's shoulder.
* You in the bath.
* You on the bed.
* You on the sofa next to a teddy that's bigger than you.
* You with mummy's pregnant friend.
* You with daddy's friend that doesn't like babies.
* You, out of focus, in your new car seat, wearing the hat great-granny's friend knitted.

The list is endless. Parents will try to capture every fleeting moment of your early life, so you might as well give them something to get really excited about – your very first smile!

The only trouble is that when you do eventually manage it there's always some know-it-all standing by who'll say, 'That wasn't a real smile, it was just wind.' Ah well, you can't win them all.

10 PULL DADDY'S CHEST HAIR TILL HE SCREAMS

Did you know that daddy's voice goes really high if you grab a handful of hair on his chest and pull? Hearing him scream like that can be a bit scary, so make sure you start yelling too – you're the most important one, remember. If you're lucky, mummy will tell him off for making such a fuss.

Speaking of mummy, why not grab her earrings next time she's giving you a cuddle? Or, failing that, the little curly bits of hair at the side of her face . . . that should give her an idea of what daddy was going on about.

And remember, these essential grabbing skills come in really useful during your first Christmas – just a firm pull on a branch of the tree and it should come down in one go.

11 WITNESS SOMETHING IMPORTANT BEFORE YOU ARE ABLE TO REMEMBER IT

Perhaps you met someone amazing today – a Hollywood movie star, the Prime Minister, or even the Pope? Or maybe you attended an important event, such as the FA Cup final or a royal wedding? Well, try and enjoy the moment now, because in a minute's time you won't remember a thing.

If you're a first child, your parents will probably go out of their way to take you to amazing places and give you incredible experiences, no matter what it costs or how far you have to travel. More experienced parents will just give you an old tin and a wooden spoon to play with. Not only is it cheaper, but they also know they can pretend you had a fantastic time abroad and simply explain that the camera was broken until you were four.

The truth is, you won't remember that round-the-world cruise or the time you went to a celebrity's birthday party. Your first memory will probably be something like dancing on your daddy's feet while saying you don't like peas, or the time a pile of chairs fell on top of you at playgroup. In short, you won't remember how daddy won a million pounds on the lottery, but you will recall the time he fell into a pile of stinging nettles while wearing only his underpants. Memory's funny like that.

12 GET A SUNTAN

There's nothing like a golden tan for making you look great and giving you that gorgeous just-back-from-holiday glow. It really is the best way to give your looks a boost – that must-have tawny colour will make your eyes sparkle and your teeth look whiter than ever (if you've got any teeth yet, that is). More importantly, your tan is a great conversation starter, giving mummy the chance to interact with other parents. Listen as they tell her, 'You know, for the under-ones you really should be using a zinc-based sunblock', or, 'I'm reporting you to Social Services'.

Here's how to join the 'brownies':

* When you're out and about, chuck your hat and socks out of the buggy to maximize the effect of the sun's rays – best to do this when mummy's not looking.

* Your skin will turn a pretty pink. But don't worry, it will turn brown in a day or two – or it will peel off. If mummy and daddy are new to parenting they'll rush you to A&E, fearing you've contracted a deadly virus. The doctor will coolly point out you've simply acquired a builder's tan and therefore they are bad parents. If they are more experienced they will start blaming one another: 'What do you mean you forgot the sun lotion? You didn't forget the lager, though, did you?' (In short, the more tanned you are, the more disapproving looks your parents will get, so it's worth the effort.)

* Get a few white Babygros to form your summer capsule wardrobe and really show off your hard-earned colour.

13 FALL IN LOVE WITH YOUR OWN REFLECTION

Looking at yourself in the mirror is an excellent way to spend the day. Here are some things to try:

* Smile.
* Smile when the baby in the mirror smiles back.
* Go 'aaaah'.
* Watch the baby go 'aaaah'.
* Play peek-a-boo: turn away from the mirror, then turn back quickly to check the baby's still there.
* Take a closer look at the baby. Press your nose right up against the mirror. Look into the baby's eyes. Fall in love.
* Notice the strange grown-up holding the baby. He reminds you of someone – why's he pulling that face?
* Ignore the man and kiss the baby in the mirror.

AGED 0-1 YEARS

14 GET A GIRLFRIEND/ BOYFRIEND

If mummy and daddy have friends with a child of a similar age and the opposite sex to you, they'll joke that you'll probably marry one another when you're older. It's probably best to humour them for the time being – you don't want to offend anyone at this early stage by telling them 'I could do better'.

The grown-ups will take lots of photographs of the two of you together – they'll think it's great fun to put you both in the bath or a cot at the same time. Then one of the daddies will say that he'd better not find you under a duvet together in sixteen years' time, or there'll be trouble . . . and they'll all have a really good laugh.

As soon as you're old enough to start speaking, it might be a good idea to point out to mummy and daddy's friends that perhaps they should get married themselves before they start pairing their children off. That'll make them go quiet for a bit.

15 ROLL OFF THE BED

This one's going to hurt. But don't worry – it'll hurt mummy a lot more than it'll hurt you.

For maximum surprise, make this the first time you have ever rolled over. And it'll have to be a double roll. This is because mummy will have exercised her responsibilities to the letter and will have put you in the middle of the bed, where she's convinced you're safe.

Before proceeding, ensure certain conditions are in place:

* Mummy must be on the loo.
* Daddy must be in the room next door or in the room directly below.
* They should both have a hangover.

No one has ever actually seen a baby roll off the bed, but this is thought to be the most successful way:

1. Rock gently from side to side, gradually building up momentum.
2. Go for it! Roll over!
3. Roll over again.
4. Fall off the bed (making a deadening thump).

A number of things will now happen:

1. Mummy will charge into the room pulling up her knickers, possibly in tears.

2. You will start screaming. But not immediately! There is a belief among the parental community that 'if they're crying, they're all right'. A heart-stopping pause of ten seconds, or until mummy picks you up, must be observed.

3. Cry even more.

4. Daddy will then casually stroll in, holding a newspaper and muttering, 'Did I hear something a minute ago?'

5. Mummy will pass you to daddy who will make funny faces at you – it is now all right for you to smile.

6. Daddy will pull a different funny face at mummy, which says, 'I'm disappointed in you.'

7. Daddy will resume reading the newspaper, while mummy tells you she'll never let you out of her sight again/she's sorry she was reading *Heat* on the loo.

Note: things will balance out between your parents in a couple of years' time when daddy forgets to strap you into your buggy and accidentally flips you out on to the road.

16 EAT OUT OF THE DOG'S BOWL

The world really opens up once you start crawling. It gives you the chance to check out hitherto unseen areas of the house. You'll soon discover that chicken-flavoured dog food's nice, but the beef's a bit dodgy – just suck off the jelly and leave the meaty chunks. Don't bother with the dried stuff though – it might be nutritious, but it wreaks havoc on your gums.

Top tip: if you haven't got a dog, or any pet, then make the food-recycling bin your first stop. It always contains some delicious treats.

Once you get started, there are plenty of other ways to tickle your tastebuds and enhance the weaning experience. Why not . . .

* Lick the railings at the zoo?
* Suck the edge of a greasy tablecloth in a café?
* Swap dummies with that runny-nosed baby in the doctor's surgery?
* Run your tongue along the edge of a park bench?
* See what the handle of a shopping trolley tastes like?
* Suck the bristles of the big brush that's kept by the toilet?

The possibilities are endless.

Your mummy's reaction to all this very much depends on whether or not you have older brothers or sisters. If you're her first child, she'll hose you down with anti-bacterial spray and scrape your tongue clean with a wet wipe. If you're not, she'll probably dab your mouth half-heartedly with the edge of her cardie while she carries on chatting to her mate.

17 MAKE SLEEP TRAINING MORE INTERESTING

While it's fine for daddy to fall asleep on the sofa in front of the telly every night, apparently it's important for children to have a proper night-time routine. Liven things up by checking out some basic Dos and Don'ts:

* **Do make sure you've got a special toy or blanket to sleep with.** Don't be palmed off with a white muslin cloth – these come in packs of twelve and are very easy to replace. Ideally, your bedtime buddy will be handmade, very expensive and only available in a special boutique in Paris. (Note: Eurostar are doing some very good deals on day trips to Paris.)

* **Don't limit the bedtime routine to the house.** Getting mummy to drive you round and round the M25 is a great way to help you drop off, and it improves her driving skills too.

* **Do rub your head on the cot mattress throughout the evening.** It helps pass the time and ensures you develop a pleasing little bald patch.

* **Don't get into the routine of sleeping in your cot.** It'll be a tough habit to break – much better to spend the evening lying on top of daddy's tummy.

* **Do convince daddy that you can't fall asleep unless he sings** 'My Bonnie Lies Over The Ocean' over and over again, while you hold on to his little finger.

18 BE THE EXCUSE USED BY YOUR PARENTS

Before you can talk – and maybe when you can talk but are out of earshot – your parents will use you as the reason they can't go to boring social events with people they don't like. For instance:

* 'I'm so sorry we can't come to your Eurovision Song Contest party – I've even made an Eiffel Tower hat – but the baby's got a temperature and I'd be too worried to leave him.'

* 'We've been looking forward to coming to your choral recital all day, but Amelie has suddenly developed a funny rash and I think I should stay at home to keep an eye on it.'

* 'I'm afraid we can't come to your primal-scream rebirthing event. Jamie's got cholera. No, it's not too bad – he should be in nursery on Monday.'

Mummy and daddy will never have enjoyed a takeaway curry and bottle of beer in front of *The X Factor* more.

Note: try not to laugh or sound as though you're having fun in the background while your parent is on the phone making their excuse. Either stay silent or whimper slightly.

Top tip: *encourage your parents to keep a log of the lies they tell on the phone, so they don't make the same excuse twice.*

19 READ A BOOK UPSIDE DOWN

If you want to impress daddy, just hold a book, any book – apparently it means you're very clever and will go to university. It doesn't matter that it's upside down or you're taking bites out of the paper – you're definitely a real brainbox and will be able to pay off his mortgage when you're older.

If she's in a playful mood, mummy will make you pop on a pair of outsized glasses to maximize the swotty effect, before taking a photograph of you 'reading' the book. She'll find the photograph in twenty years' time and wonder why you're dressed up as Elton John – or the bloke with glasses from *Big Cook, Little Cook*.

20 CRAWL ACROSS A DIRTY FLOOR IN A WHITE BABYGRO

Soon after you learn to crawl, daddy will be dying to show off your new skill to visiting friends. For some reason, mummy won't be so keen. She'll try to stop daddy, but it's no good – he's on a roll. Here's what will happen:

1. Daddy will proudly announce to the other grown-ups that they must see 'what the baby's just learnt to do'.

2. He'll place you on the kitchen floor. You'll be wearing your new white Babygro.

3. You will obediently scamper across the floor .

4. Guests will applaud.

5. Daddy will lift you up.

6. Everyone will quietly clock the black greasy marks on your hands and knees, and the week-old fried egg stuck to your leg.

7. Guests will try and talk about something else, but their eyes will be darting around to see where mummy keeps the Hoover/floor mop – or, in fact, if she owns any cleaning equipment at all.

8. Mummy will look flushed.

9. Guests will wonder it it's safe to eat here.

Note: you'll be wearing navy-blue Babygros from now on. It's a lot less hassle than cleaning the kitchen floor.

AGED 1-2 YEARS
THE EMOTIONAL TODDLING DAYS

Christopher Columbus discovered America, and Newton discovered gravity when an apple fell on his head, but you'll discover far more interesting things this year. Things such as a simple bottom-shuffling technique that'll get you from A to B without you having to bother with all that walking malarkey; the rigid body position that's been proved to prevent 97 per cent of adults from clipping a baby into a buggy; and random fun activities like tipping the contents of the food-recycling bin into a basket of clean washing.

Feel free to experiment because you've just reached what is known in the parenting game as the 'into-everything stage'. When you come across an object you've never seen before, you'll quickly learn to do one of three things: eat it, open it or knock it over. And remember, mummy's the one to blame when you're discovered sliding off the kitchen counter covered in olive oil. She'll soon learn to keep a closer eye on you.

This is the year you'll run before you can walk, flush the toilet before you're out of nappies and scribble on the walls before you can hold a crayon properly. Make sure you have a fantastic time. Pull out all the drawers, slide your fingers into the jamb of every door and yank any animal's tail – soon your parents will learn how to 'toddler-proof' your home. But remember, you'll have to show them how to open those kiddie locks on the kitchen cupboards and how the stairgate works – they won't have a clue.

21 FIND YOUR LOST SOCK ON SOME RAILINGS

If you lose a favourite sock on the way to the park, don't bother scouring the gutters for it on the way home – check out the railings instead.

There's an unwritten law among grown-ups that if they find a stray sock or glove in the street, they will stick it on the spike of some railings.

The grown-up will flatten the sock nicely, then slide it over the spike. If they pick up a lost glove, they'll arrange the fingers to look as though it's a hand waving at you. Doesn't it look funny!

Note: if there are no railings within a 20m radius of where the sock has been found, a low wall will be used instead.

Top tip: *no one will nick a stray sock or glove, to be honest, it's no use to anyone – but other items of clothing would be considered fair game.*

22 PLAY WITH THE BOX THAT A BIG, EXPENSIVE TOY CAME IN

You can climb into it, hide in it, scribble on it and get someone to drag you around in it. What's more, it looks great in any living room. Why not put it right in front of the telly?

Tip: *the more you want to play with the box, the more daddy will encourage you to play with the toy that was inside it. He'll explain it cost a lot of money and will offer to play with you and your new toy for as much time as you like – as long as you stop playing with the box. Play with the box for a bit longer. Daddy will still be waiting after you've finished.*

If you haven't got a box, or if yours has disappeared and mummy says she's no idea where it's gone, you'll just have to amuse yourself with daddy's keys or mobile phone. They're far better to play with than toys.

Note: savvy parents don't actually buy small children any toys. They just give them the empty boxes they get from the supermarket.

23 MAKE WASHING-POWDER MOUNTAINS

There's amazing stuff under the kitchen sink, but washing powder's the best. It pours beautifully, and then makes lovely mountain shapes on the kitchen floor.

Hold the box up high and watch the contents slowly trickle out. Let the powder run free and find its own level. To the untrained eye this might look like you're simply wasting four quid's worth of soap powder, but you know you're being taught a complex lesson in geometry – for instance, discovering that every point on a cone is connected to the vertex. Or something.

If there is any left after you have created your washing-powder mountain, try scattering it around the floor like freshly fallen snow. It feels lovely. Then why not lie on your back in the snow and sweep your arms and legs up and down to create a stunning washing-powder-angel shape? Mummy won't believe her eyes.

24 BRIGHTEN UP A BORING WEDDING

The easiest way to do this is to play with the gravel outside the main door of wherever the wedding's taking place. The way you get from the wedding to the gravel is as follows:

1. Start by making cooing noises as the bride enters. (If it is a commitment ceremony or civil partnership, both parties will probably walk in together – if so then this is when you should start cooing.)

2. As the service gets underway, begin to cry softly. A parent will lift you up and try to calm you down.

3. Struggle and cry more loudly. Look at the irritated faces of those around you as you wipe your snotty nose on your parent's shoulder.

4. As the couple recite their vows you can really go for it by shouting, 'No! No! No!' A parent will now swiftly remove you – it's usually daddy, because he won't have spent as much on his outfit.

5. Go outside and start playing with the gravel.

Note: grown-ups think gravel is just a mixture of tiny rocks and stones. But you know it's actually a smorgasbord of colours, shapes, sizes and textures. No two pieces are alike, and some of them are diamonds!

So now here's what you do:

1. Grab a few handfuls of gravel and spread it all out on the steps.

2. Lie down and start sorting it into groups – the tiniest bits together, the shiniest ones together, and so on. Take your time – weddings drag on for ages.

3. Pick your favourite piece. Lick it to see what it looks like when it's wet.

4. As the newly married couple walk down the steps after the ceremony, quickly gather up the gravel and pop it into daddy's pocket ... mind his camera!

5. If you are a bridesmaid or pageboy you will now be required to have some photographs taken.

Finally, you must try to rest your voice for a bit ... you're going to need it during the speeches later on.

25 FLUSH SOMETHING VALUABLE DOWN THE TOILET

Just because you're not toilet-trained, it doesn't mean you can't use the loo in some way. Next time mummy's back is turned for one moment, why not carry out a few experiments? You'll soon discover it's the greatest toy ever ... especially if mummy's on a water meter.

The two best things about playing with the toilet are:

1. The splash you get when you drop an item in the water.
2. The way the item disappears for ever as soon as you've pushed down on the handle or pressed the little button on the top of the loo. Better go and get something else to drop in there!

The two worst things about playing with the toilet are:

1. Mummy's face when she discovers you've flushed her engagement ring down the loo. Probably best not to mention that you pulled the chain on your christening bracelet at the same time.
2. Daddy's face when he discovers you've flushed his electric razor down the lav. Tell him to calm down – a qualified plumber will be able to retrieve it from the S-bend simply by removing the toilet.

Enjoy the loo now, while you can. Next year you'll probably want to develop a phobia about it.

26 CREATE A BATHTIME HAIRSTYLE

Banish bad-hair days and experiment with some great new styles the next time you have your hair washed. Just lather up and get mummy or daddy to work on these fab looks:

* 'LITTLE DEVIL' – part your hair, then sweep up each half in a horn shape on top of your head.

* 'UNICORN' – simply sweep all your hair into a horn at the front of your head.

* 'MOHICAN' – smooth your hair into a punky ridge running down the middle of your head.

* 'CUTESY' – swirl some tendrils of hair into sweet, face-framing kiss-curls.

* 'THE INTERVIEW LOOK' – create a low side parting, then tuck the shorter side behind your ear and smooth the rest. (**Note:** pull the hair further down your forehead to create the hilarious 'Hitler look'.)

27 GIVE MUMMY A BLACK EYE

At some stage or other you will accidentally wallop mummy in the face with a hard object, and give her what is known in medical circles as a 'shiner'. You are most likely to hit her with one of the following:

* The remote control for the telly.
* A toy car.
* The pointed foot of a Barbie doll.
* Your sippy cup – watch out you don't spill Ribena on her new white jeans!
* Her mobile phone.

Mummy will cry but don't worry, she'll soon stop her hysterical shouts of 'I'm blind, I'm blind' – so long as you play your part...

CRY LIKE YOU'VE BEEN SNATCHED BY A GYPSY!

Although noisy, this is the quickest way to help mummy regain her perspective.

However, it is possible that mummy might actually be in a little bit of pain, so make amends by offering to go with her to the hospital. After the three-hour wait, you could helpfully declutter her bag while she shows the doctor her bruise. How she'll laugh when she looks down to find her condoms, Weight Watchers' registration card and packet of fags neatly arranged around the doctor's feet.

28 SLIP HALFWAY OUT OF A HIGH CHAIR

Scientists say that a newborn baby can hang on to the edge of a cliff by its fingertips for the first ten hours after it's born. It's unlikely your parents tested this theory, but they'll always wonder if it is actually possible. Well, you might be one year old now, but it's not too late to demonstrate your iron grip next time daddy forgets to strap you into your high chair.

Maybe daddy's just being slapdash, or perhaps he thinks your tummy's chunky enough to wedge you into the chair. Anyway, don't point out his mistake. Just bide your time till the doorbell goes or he needs the loo – then go for it!

1. Shuffle your bottom down to the edge of the chair – the mashed banana you spat out earlier should act as a lubricant . . . off you go!

2. Hang on to the arms of the chair for dear life – your legs should be dangling midair and your face should be pressed up against the underside of the tray.

3. Scream as loudly as you can. It will sound a bit muffled, but this adds to the sense of danger.

4. Daddy will come running into the room. He will pause for a moment or two to admire the sheer strength of your grip.

5. Daddy will save you and he will even give you ice cream for pudding.

29 LAUGH OPENLY AT A NAKED ADULT

Grown-ups look hilarious when they're in the nud. But when you spot mummy clambering out of the bath, or daddy pulling on his pants, don't just run out of the bathroom laughing hysterically: pause for a moment to take it all in – and then run out of the bathroom laughing hysterically.

Tip: *why not bring up the subject of mummy's big bosoms or daddy's varicose veins next time they have some friends in the house? Friends such as the postman, or the bloke who comes to read the gas meter.*

30 LOSE YOUR MOST-TREASURED POSSESSION IN A BALL-PIT

Grown-ups love going to indoor play centres, because they get to relax with a coffee and an old copy of *Grazia*, safe in the knowledge you're 'having fun'. I wonder how they'd like to drag themselves out of a shoulder-height pit full of plastic balls while someone twice their size is hurtling towards them on a commando swing?

So, the simple technique of losing your most-treasured possession is guaranteed to shake them out of their stupor.

Top tip: *ideally this should be very small and the thing you have to take to bed with you every night. A tiny fluffy mouse the size of your thumb is ideal. Let's call him Mousie.*

What to do:

1. Sneak Mousie out of the house – down your pants or under the buggy liner is ideal. Only reveal him once you get to the play centre.

2. Take Mousie into the ball-pit with you, promising faithfully you won't lose him.

3. Wander around aimlessly for ten minutes, and then put Mousie down. Move away from him and go about your business, making sure you visit every part of the ball-pit.

4. Timing is essential here. Wait until everyone has their coats on, and then announce you've lost Mousie in the ball-pit. Tell them you have no idea where you put him. Start to cry, saying you'll never be able to sleep tonight.

5. Start hunting – extra points if they have to go through one of those overhead Perspex tunnels. Point out that you're hungry and a few Smileys might help ease your rumbling tum.

6. On average, it'll take mummy or daddy three hours to locate Mousie – he's usually in the back corner of the ball-pit in which someone's had a wee.

31 MAKE THEM WONDER IF YOU WERE SWITCHED AT BIRTH

Why not plant the seed of doubt that you were switched at birth ... with the baby belonging to the strange woman in the hospital bed next to mummy's?

It's not the good stuff that'll make mummy and daddy worry. A sudden ability to draw, a facility with another language or a prodigious talent for music would all be happily accepted as skills you've inherited from them – along with your cute dimples and big blue eyes. It's the odd stuff that'll unsettle them. Try doing some funny blinking for a day or two, making a weird grunting sound while you're drinking your milk or developing a short-lived twitch.

Granny will be the first to say it: 'We've never had anything like that in our family. It must've come from the other side.' Then it's nana's turn: 'We've never had anything like that in our family. It must've come from the other side.' Mummy and daddy will start looking worried. You'll hear mummy confess that she did fall asleep in hospital just after you were born – but only for a bit; daddy will start pacing up and down talking about something called DNA.

This is the time to come running into the room with your nappy on your head. See the smile appear on daddy's face when granny says, 'Look at that – just like your daddy!'

32 WEAR FOOD AS A FASHION ACCESSORY

Raspberries have been cleverly designed to fit perfectly on to the tips of your fingers. They also have the added benefit of leaving a lovely red colour that looks just like nail polish. This red stuff (or juice) is ideal for colouring and, unlike the coloured pencils mummy has been giving you, is tricky to get off.

You could also try these foodie dressing-up tricks:

* A pair of cherries on stalks doubles as a stunning earring – just loop it over the top of your ear.

* Hula Hoops make stylish rings for little fingers.

* Strawberries can be rubbed over your mouth as lipstick.

* Squirt tomato ketchup on your face and pretend you've injured yourself. To maximize the effect, lie at the bottom of the stairs and scream.

* You can fashion soggy Weetabix into a wig and leave it on top of your head to dry.

* Rub flour all over your body to achieve a scary ghost effect!

33 NICK SOMETHING FROM A SHOP

It's a sad fact of life that most toddlers steal at one time or another. Not just small toys from other people's houses, but stuff from shops too. This is called 'shoplifting'.

These are the top three items nicked by the under-twos:

1. Sweeties from the pick & nicks – sorry, pick & mix – in a newsagent.
2. Chocolate bars displayed around the till area in supermarkets – these goodies are at buggy height, so mummy won't notice you helping yourself.
3. Free gifts from the front of comics at the cornershop.

When she finds out what you've been up to, mummy will take you back to the shop, where she will apologize to the shopkeeper and offer to pay for the bag of pear drops you took. On the way home, she'll try to explain that even though you're too young to know the difference between right and wrong, you must stop stealing . . . otherwise next time the police may have to get involved. This is the perfect time to ask her why daddy always comes home from work with rolls and rolls of Sellotape and lots of packets of Post-it notes in his bag – isn't that stealing? Mummy will go a bit red at this point and happily buy you whatever you want.

34 GET AWAY FROM IT ALL

Every child needs a place of their own. Somewhere they can kick back and relax.

The great news is that a home-from-home can be found anywhere – behind the curtains in the living room, inside a wardrobe, or in the narrow gap between your shed and next door's fence. But remember to keep it secret!

Next time mummy's not looking – perhaps when she's engrossed in the latest copy of *Heat* – head for your den and hunker down. Take your favourite cuddly toys and a few snacks with you. Why not have a little nap?

It's good fun to keep really quiet when you realize mummy's looking for you ... this game's called Hide and Seek. You'll hear her check the front door, then run around every room in the house before checking the front door again. She'll start calling for you – doesn't her voice sound funny?! Perhaps she'll say things to herself such as:

* 'Why did I think the Boden online sale was more important than looking after my son?'
* 'I'm a terrible mother.'
* 'I promise never to shout at her again, even when she drinks from the toilet, so long as she's safe.'

Wait till she's about to call the police, then suddenly reappear. Look at the expression on mummy's face! She'll hug you tight, kiss you, and then tell you off. Then she'll kiss you again. Don't worry ... she's going to be fine.

35 BE CLINGY

A great way to show mummy how much you love her is to go through a clingy phase. Follow these tips and you'll really reassure her that you'll never ever let her go:

* Get cosy. Squeeze into the tiny space next to her on a chair, offering to turn the pages of her magazine. If she's sitting on a sofa, climb up behind her, wrapping your arms tightly around her neck.

* Run a toy car up and down her arm, or get your dolly to jump on her lap and give her lots of kisses while she's trying to watch telly.

* Follow her around like a puppy, so whenever she turns round she'll trip over you.

* Pretend you're her shadow by standing on the back of her slippers or hanging on to her legs, so she has to shuffle around the house while she's doing her chores.

* Be loyal to mummy. Refuse to interact with anyone – family members as well as strangers – apart from her. Sit on her lap during all social occasions, including playgroups.

* Build up her muscles by getting her to carry you everywhere.

* Never leave her alone. Insist on going everywhere with her, including the loo.

36 RIDE ON EVERYTHING

You've cruised the supermarket shopping aisles in a trolley and you've trundled up the garden in a wheelbarrow, but it doesn't have to stop there – if it's got wheels, handles or can be dragged along the floor, you can have a free ride on it.

Imagine a regular day at home. Mummy might be doing the hoovering – why not hop on and have a ride? Perhaps she's pegging out some washing – that's an empty laundry basket she's bringing in from the garden which could have you in it! Maybe she's dragging the bins out for recycling – why not sit on top? These are just for starters.

Sit on a suitcase at the airport, clamber into that beach bag, or hop into granny's shopping buggy. Ride on the conveyor belt in a supermarket, climb on to the squeegee while mummy's mopping the floor, or get inside an empty box and make someone push you around.

And when the grown-up says, 'That's enough, get off', remember what to say: 'Just one more go . . . pleeeeeeease.'

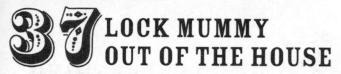

37 LOCK MUMMY OUT OF THE HOUSE

You think you know mummy – but do you really? A true test of mummy's character is to find out how she copes in a crisis. Why not slam the door shut on her next time she's bringing in the shopping? She'll quickly realize she's locked out without her keys, purse or mobile phone – and that you're inside.

Top tip: *cry loudly to make her stress levels rocket.*

Now sit back and observe. The way mummy reacts will say a lot about her personality type, and may give you some clues to how you're going to turn out. Does she:

* Poke a long stick through the letterbox to retrieve the set of keys she's hung on the wall so they're out of your reach? Mummy's a STRATEGIST. She uses clear, logical thinking to solve a problem.

* Smash a window and clamber through, trailing glass everywhere? Mummy's a NATURAL LEADER. She'll do the big stuff and get someone else to clear up her mess later.

* Calmly walk into the garden to get the spare set of keys she keeps under the rabbit hutch? Mummy's a REALIST. She knew this would happen one day.

* Sit on the doorstep and patiently wait for daddy, saying he'll be home from work soon? Mummy's an IDEALIST. Of course daddy won't be home soon – he's forgotten to tell her he's going to the pub after work.

38 ANSWER THE PHONE

This is a win-win situation for everyone. You love to answer the phone and the person on the other end loves hearing you answer it. However, you need to make sure your phone manner is right. Here's what to do when it rings:

1. Get to the phone first, pick it up and say 'Hello?'
2. Say 'Hello?' again.
3. The person on the other end of the line will ask to speak to mummy or daddy. That tremor in their voice is them 'being patient'.
4. Say 'Hello?' again.
5. Start to throw in random comments such as, 'I done a poo,' 'Teddy gone' or 'Uh-oh!'

Now you have two choices – either leave the phone off the hook and wander off without mentioning the call to anyone, or carefully replace the receiver.

Don't worry. It might ring again soon and you'll get another chance to answer it.

39 GET OUT OF YOUR COT EVEN WHEN YOU'RE WEARING A GROBAG

Imagine the scene: mummy slumped on the sofa with a glass of wine in front of a programme about moving to the country, safe in the knowledge you're trapped . . . sorry, secure . . . in your cot. See the look on her face when you suddenly appear – triumphant – at the sitting-room door.

Unless you start working out how to deal with the 'Grobag problem' now, you're facing a lot of nights of you alone in your cot with only Bunny for company. Grobags with poppers or Velcro are easy to get out of. If you're not so lucky, yours will have a zip.

If you've already built up a reputation as a 'climber', mummy will put you into an inside-out Grobag – so it's zipped up from the inside. If this is the case then you're stuck and you're going to have to learn to walk in it – at least this'll come in useful for your first sack race on sports day.

So, if you're a 'climber', chuck a blanket on to the floor to break your fall and then flip yourself out of your cot. Make your way quietly towards the sitting-room – either by shuffling along while still inside the Grobag, or trailing it behind you like a superhero cloak. Pause for a moment and enjoy looking at mummy in her relaxed state before she realizes you're there. Doesn't she look sweet?

40 'LIVE-HEAD' THE FLOWERS IN GRANNY'S GARDEN

If granny hasn't got many toys for you to play with, you'll just have to find something else to do – and 'live-heading' flowers fits the bill perfectly. Only fill your pockets with the biggest and most perfect blooms . . . you don't want to bother with the dead bits.

You could also:

* Take a bite out of every apple in her fruit bowl before carefully returning them biteside-down.

* Use your thumbnail to make pretty patterns on the leaves of her prize rubber plant. They'll seem subtle at first, but will become more defined as the leaves start to age.

* Rearrange her collection of fridge magnets that she's brought back from every single holiday over the last thirty years. Slide the best ones into the 5mm dusty gap between the fridge and the cupboard.

* Settle down to eat the contents of the sugar bowl.

You'll be having fun while granny is catching up with mummy and daddy. Don't worry – she won't discover what you've been up to until after you've gone.

AGED 2-3 YEARS
HAVE SOME 'ME, ME, ME' TIME

Perhaps you've already heard about the 'terrible twos'. Unfortunately, it's true – both mummy and daddy can be terrible this year, which is a shame as they're always on at you to have some manners. The best thing is to ignore them, because you don't want your parents to spoil this precious 'me, me, me' time. Failing that, if mummy keeps on asking you, 'What's the magic word?', tell her it's 'abracadabra'.

This is the year to experiment and be adventurous in everything you do. Try sliding headfirst down the banisters with a bucket on your head, or rubbing margarine all over the new sofa. It doesn't matter what you do, as long as you do it by yourself . . . without any help from anyone else. Don't worry about how long it takes you to put your shoes on, or on which foot you put them – if mummy's late for work, she's late for work; it's as simple as that.

The main thing is to keep 'em guessing. Be super-clingy with mummy one minute, then push her away the next; dawdle for hours on a simple trip to the postbox on the corner, then make an unexpected run for it when daddy lets you out of your buggy in the supermarket. Like with a packet of Revels, they'll never know what's coming next.

The truth is, it really doesn't matter what you get up to this year or who you offend because, like the drunk who wakes up in the morning with a traffic cone on his head, you won't remember a thing. Enjoy it while you can!

41 HAVE FUN ON THE NAUGHTY STEP

Definition: 'naughty step', noun, the boring place a small child is sent to when they've done something naughty. The classic naughty step is the bottom stair in a family home, where a grown-up is able to exert discipline while simultaneously cooking the tea. However, any step can be used – for instance, the kerb in front of a betting shop or the ledge outside a pub.

If you've had the bad luck to be banished to the naughty step by a cross grown-up, time can really drag, so it's essential to find something interesting to do...

* Clever babies always have something up their sleeve – literally. Hide a small doll or toy car about your person at all times, so you've got something to play with secretly while you're grounded. Check out the new style of shoe where you can stash toys in the heel – just slip the shoe off and lift the insole to access them. There may be room in there for a small snack too.

* If you're not so lucky as to have any hidden goodies, go with the limited options available: pick your nose, or run your nail along a wallpaper seam until the paper lifts away from the wall – see how many bits you can peel off before the grown-up comes back.

* Exercise your vocal cords with a song. Make sure it sounds as mournful as possible to ensure maximum grown-up guilt. If you can't do sad, do repetitive.

42 GET SOMETHING STUCK UP YOUR NOSE

The inside of your nose is like Dr Who's TARDIS – it's much bigger in there than it appears from the outside. Why not see what everyday objects you can fit up your nozzle? Everyone tries it – once.

Top 10 Things to Stick Up Your Nose

1. A pea.
2. A peanut.
3. A Polly Pocket shoe.
4. A marble.
5. The vital piece of daddy's watch, kept on the mantelpiece till he gets round to mending it.
6. The dog playing piece from your Monopoly set.
7. The end of a lipsalve.
8. A button.
9. A bead.
10. An olive (stuffed).

Top 5 Ways to Get an Object Out of Your Nose

1. Blowing into a hankie.
2. Mummy sucking it out of your nostril.
3. Going to the doctor.
4. A magnet (only if a ball bearing is stuck up your nose).
5. Invasive surgery (this can involve ice cream).

AGED 2-3 YEARS

43 BREAK A DVD PLAYER

Next time daddy's removing his *World at War* disc from the DVD player, watch carefully to find out which button causes the small tray to pop out. When daddy leaves the room, take the time to familiarize yourself with this process – over and over again. If you pull the tray hard enough, you might be able to get it out in one go. Failing that, why not work out what you can put on top of the tray to feed into the machine? This is trickier than it sounds, because the DVD player's slim slot poses more of a challenge to today's child than the old-style video recorder's letterbox-sized mouth did to previous generations.

Tip: *a large rice cake fits perfectly. Give it a quick suck around the edges before putting it on the tray, to make sure it sticks.*

Beads, flower heads and the sponge from inside mummy's powder compact are also worth trying. The humble jam sandwich, cut up nice and small, can usually be relied upon to work. You might have to squash it down a bit though.

Super tip: *it's worth ambling off in the other direction when daddy accusingly asks, 'Have you been messing with this machine again?'*

44 WIN MEDALS AND CERTIFICATES

It took rower Steve Redgrave nearly twenty years to win just five Olympic gold medals. And Stephen Hawking notched up a measly six certificates in forty years. But these days any self-respecting toddler will have received a dozen such prizes during their first term at nursery. That's because at the moment practically everything you do can win you something. For example:

* Good colouring in at playgroup? Certificate.
* Had a day out at a theme park? Medal.
* Was a shepherd in the Nativity play? Medal.
* New pair of shoes? Certificate.
* Dental appointment? Medal.
* Raised 73 pence for nursery in a sponsored walk? Certificate.

Medals are slightly more sought after because you can put them on teddy when you get home. What's more, they're probably made from real gold, so you could swap them for a house when you're older.

Other children's parents are always happy to congratulate you on acquiring your latest medal – unless it's for winning *Junior Mastermind* or passing piano grade 8. Then they go a bit quiet.

45 MAKE A MAGIC POTION

While away an afternoon by creating a magic potion. If you get the recipe just right, it might turn you invisible.

You'll need a large container, like a bucket, washing-up bowl or one of daddy's shoes. Here's what you do . . .

1. Pour some mud or sand into your container. Stir it with a big twig while at the same time adding some liquid – puddle-water's ideal.

2. Now add any other ingredients you fancy – soggy leaves, pinecones, flowers or bits of gravel are good.

3. Garnish it with a squirt of sunscreen, food colouring or mummy's Chanel No. 5.

4. Give the whole thing a final stir before dragging the container into the sun so the mixture can simmer gently. Watch out for those splashes!

5. Give it a name – 'stinky pie' is always a popular choice. The potion will then need a couple of hours to develop fully, so go inside and watch the telly.

6. Forget all about it for four and a half weeks.

7. Mummy will eventually find the potion, and just as she is about to pour it down the drain, you go absolutely crazy, telling her you were 'just about to play with that'.

8. Drag some teddies out for a 'potion picnic'. Sit them around the container, taking care to prop them up nicely – or they'll fall nose-first into it.

Note: with care, a potion can last for several years.

46 LIKE THE RABBITS BEST AT THE ZOO

Mummy and daddy love the idea of exposing you to nature. And nothing makes them laugh more after spending £36 on tickets to the zoo than your favourite animal being something you could see in next door's hutch.

So, when asked the question, 'Which animal did you like best?', simply say 'the rabbits'.

You will now be faced with a number of questions and zoological facts:

> **Them:** But didn't you like the cheetahs? They can run at 70mph.
>
> **You:** Rabbits.
>
> **Them:** What about the elephants? They weigh 8 tonnes.
>
> **You:** Rabbits.
>
> **Them:** You must have liked the giraffes? They can be 22ft tall.
>
> **You:** Rabbits.

An added benefit to this approach is that you will actually get more trips to the zoo in future – mummy and daddy never like being proved wrong.

47 GET MUMMY A ROW OF SEATS ON AN AEROPLANE

Mummy shouldn't have to pay for business class on an aeroplane to get the room you require – she needs that extra money to buy comics and stickers. So, unless you want to be squashed next to a disapproving fat man for a few hours, you and mummy have got to work together.

Make sure you're travelling with an airline that has done away with seat numbers – which means it's 'first come, first served'. Watch how fast mummy can push your buggy to the front of the queue! Hold on tight – there's not enough time to bother with buckles and straps.

Once you're on board, plonk yourselves down in a nice empty row of seats and make yourselves at home. The trick now is to prevent anyone else from sitting with you. You're not allowed to say, 'Go away, you smell' – you'll have to be a bit cleverer. You could try any of the following:

* Go along with mummy when she says things like, 'Oh, darling, I hope you're not going to be sick again', even though you're feeling absolutely fine. Clever mummy.
* Start crying hysterically. The louder, the better.
* If you're all cried out from the journey to the airport, try singing a song. Over and over again.
* Sit down and start kicking the seats in front of you – this way you'll end up with two rows to yourself.

Once the doors shut, sit back and enjoy the flight!

48 BE A FUNNY EATER

Sweets and biscuits are the nicest foods. Make sure they form the basis of your diet by becoming a funny eater.

Note: being a funny eater also gets you noticed – and every baby needs attention. Do people like Madonna because she's a brilliant singer? No. It's because she's a funny eater.

There's only one rule to being a funny eater . . .

KEEP CHANGING THE RULES!

Start by refusing to eat anything that mummy has made using more than one saucepan, or that has taken her over twenty minutes to produce, or has different food types touching one another.

Now you've cut down her options, refuse to eat anything green, or anything with lumps in it. And be careful of any food that's smooth – it might contain puréed vegetables.

You may prefer simply to limit yourself to a couple of accepted foods – for instance, pitta bread and carrots. However, insist the pitta bread is served slightly warm and cut into 1cm-width fingers. The carrots should be raw and cut into rounds – reject any carrot presented in a baton shape. One day, refuse to eat these foods as well.

Stick with it and one day mummy will be only too pleased for you to have a jam sandwich for tea – at least the jam's got fruit in it.

49 DO SOMETHING BRILLIANT FOR DADDY – BUT ONLY DO IT ONCE

The next time you get daddy by himself, why not impress him with an unusually precocious skill?

Perhaps you could count to ten in German, or do a brilliant impersonation of Homer Simpson. Before you know it, he'll yell for mummy, plonk you down in front of her and order you to do it again. This is where you look blankly at him, as though you don't know what he's talking about.

He'll ask you again, and then again. Eventually, he'll beg you. Twenty minutes later, as you wander off to play with some Lego, you'll hear him saying things like, 'But he really can do the Rubik's Cube', or 'Honestly, Liz, she actually knew it was a greater-spotted woodpecker'.

Take a look at mummy's face as you leave the room. She'll think he's gone mad.

50 CRASH DADDY'S COMPUTER

Seeing daddy working on his computer reminds you that you wanted to play on the CBeebies website. Here's how to get him off his laptop, and you on it:

AGED 2-3 YEARS

1. Go up to daddy and ask him what he's doing. He'll tell you he's working.

2. Ask if you can watch. He'll say, 'Okay, but only if you're quiet' – he has to get this report in by tomorrow or he'll lose his job.

3. Ask if you can sit on his lap. He'll agree, so long as you promise not to touch the keyboard.

4. Watch daddy type. Don't his fingers fly?! He'll laugh and say he wishes he could work at home every day – it's much more fun being with you than sitting in his boring office.

5. Ask if you can look at the CBeebies website. Daddy'll say you can in a bit when he's done the spell-check on this document. He'll remind you not to touch the keyboard.

6. Touch the keyboard.

7. Watch the computer screen go blank. Daddy will ask you to get off his lap, explaining that he's lost everything now.

8. Ask if you can play your computer games.

9. See daddy rocking backwards and forwards with his head in his hands.

10. Go and watch telly while daddy sorts out getting someone to fix his computer . . . maybe you'll be able to download those *Charlie and Lola* pictures later on.

Note: if you're too busy to complete all of the above ten stages, simply trip over the power cord.

51 WIN A WORLD RECORD FOR THE LONGEST TIME SPENT ON A SWING

A great way to let your parents burn off their excess energy is to get them down the park and make them push you on the swing for a few hours. While you're there, you might as well try to get into the *Guinness World Records* for the 'longest time spent on a swing (must be in constant motion)'. However, there are three main obstacles for any would-be record breaker in this category:

1. There are other children waiting to have 'a go'. Ignore them – you got to the swing first, remember. Ignore their pushy parent too. The one who loudly says, 'Don't worry, Charlie. That child's had a really long go and is bound to be finished soon.' That's just a tactic to get you off the swing and their kid on.

2. Your parent says their arms are tired. Use different tactics for different parents. If it's daddy, flatter him by saying his arms can't possibly be tired because he's a 'Superdaddy'. He'll be so pleased that you'll get at least another half an hour out of him. If it's mummy, tell her that her arms look lovely and slim in that new sleeveless T-shirt – it must be all the swing-pushing she's been doing recently. She'll be thrilled, especially if you say it loudly enough for all the other mummies to hear.

3. It's teatime. Start negotiating. If you're lucky, you'll be allowed to eat tea on the go. Though you'd better start praying it's sandwiches rather than spag bol – otherwise you'll just have to say you're not hungry and don't want any tea. Don't worry – mummy or daddy will be only too happy to provide you with a light, nutritious meal in the middle of the night when you wake up starving.

52 S-T-R-E-A-K!

The best way to brighten up a boring wedding is to take off all your clothes and run around the church giggling. In fact, stripping down to your birthday suit and shouting 'look at me' breaks the tension on most formal occasions.

Great Opportunities to Streak

* At any restaurant that has white tablecloths and doesn't offer a kids' menu or colouring-in utensils as standard.

* On a visit to mummy or daddy's office.

* Funerals.

* When visiting someone in hospital.

* At a dental appointment.

How to Do It

* The element of surprise is key . . . so don't tell anyone what you're planning to do.

* Timing is crucial. Neither parent should be close enough to grab you.

* Whip off your clothes and then make your break for the border – make sure your pants are completely off or they might trip you up.

* Run as fast as your legs can carry you.

* Clock the reaction on people's faces – amusement, shock, revulsion.

* A parent will start to chase after you. Try running in sharp zigzagging motions. Grown-ups are like elephants – they find it hard to change direction quickly thanks to their huge bulk.

* However, they will eventually catch you and carry you away over their shoulder like a sack of potatoes. This is a bit humiliating but worth it for the rush of adrenalin that streaking gives you.

53 BECOME A COLLECTOR

You don't need cash to be a collector. Just look around you – you can pick up great stuff everywhere for free!

Start off with the 'National Stick Collection'. Slip a few small twigs into mummy's bag when you're out and about. Over the months gather bigger and bigger sticks, till mummy eventually finds herself bringing 6ft branches back from the park on the top of your buggy.

Note: Clever adults will try persuading you to leave your sticks at the park gate 'so a dog can play with them later'. Don't fall for this trick – dog owners say similar things: 'Drop, Rover! A toddler can play with that later.'

Keep a special eye out for rubber bands – postmen casually drop them everywhere, even though they're considered a health-and-safety hazard and the postie could be sued if someone were to slip on one. By picking them up, you could help him keep his job.

As time passes, you'll notice the streets are literally paved with treasures, so keep your eyes peeled. Look out for coins, small stones that look pretty in the rain, bits of metal, old cotton buds . . . the list is endless.

Deposit your finds in the back of the buggy and never bother with them again – unless you discover your collectibles in a bin, that is. In this case you need to transfer them to mummy's handbag, where they'll be safe.

54 HAVE A WEE IN THE OPEN AIR

Toilet training sending you potty? Having a wee outside is fun and will get you some fresh air too!

The first time will probably be an accident. One minute you're crouched on the lawn looking at a snail, the next you're having a wee through your pants. Okay, you'll get a bit wet, but you'll immediately realize it's a lot less hassle than toddler wipes and hand-washing regimes.

Mummy will now take to carrying your potty around with her all the time – she'll be pleased you're not still using nappies and you'll be pleased to get to have wees in all sorts of interesting places, such as:

* Outside a café. Let other toddlers have a quick tinkle in your potty after you. Mummy's emptying it anyway, so it might as well be really, really full.

* In a shopping centre. Using your potty in the lift will allow you to meet people and wee at the same time.

* In a pod on the London Eye. Panoramic views, a nice wee – what could be more sophisticated?

Before you leave your potty days behind you, make sure you experience the ultimate outside wee ...

ON THE HARD SHOULDER OF A MOTORWAY!

An adult will be holding you. You'll get back in the car feeling much better. They'll have a wet leg. Happy days.

AGED 2-3 YEARS

55 LIVEN UP A RESTAURANT MEAL

A lovely treat for the whole family is to visit a restaurant. Mummy gets a night off from the cooking, daddy gets to impress the waiters with his knowledge of the wine list ('Second one from the top, please'), and you get to play with the hand dryers in the toilets.

Note: observe the strange change in the behaviour of mummy and daddy, compared to meal times at home. Usually when you spill your drink you get a sharp 'be careful'. In the restaurant this becomes, 'Are you all right, darling? Would you like another?' Exploit this change.

So, here are some things you can do:

* While you're waiting for the food to arrive, take a stroll across the restaurant. Stop and stare at anyone who looks interesting. Don't say anything. Just take a really close look at what they're eating.

* At last your food arrives, and it looks delicious! Now's the time to realize you need the loo again. When mummy points out you've already been three times, explain loudly you need to 'do a poo'. Mummy will glare at daddy, then daddy will escort you to the toilet. There's no need to rush – take your time in there.

* Back at the table, just eat the bits you want and slip what you don't want on to daddy's plate when he's not looking. When you all leave, blinking in the bright sunshine, you'll be amazed it's only quarter to six.

56 CALL DADDY BY HIS FIRST NAME

Did you know that your parents' first names aren't Mummy and Daddy? Apparently they were 'real people' before they had you and had proper names, like Bev and Paul, Vix and Dave, Sally and George.

Some parents are a bit coy about revealing their first names to you, but persevere, because once you find out the truth you can have some fun in public.

Just think about it. One day you'll be wandering around M&S's menswear department with daddy, while mummy's downstairs frantically trying to find something to buy to wear to a wedding. Daddy will ask your opinion about a pair of cords. You'll say, 'I think they're great . . . Steve!'

Daddy will quietly ask you not to call him Steve. You then start jumping around the shop floor shouting, 'What's the matter? Don't you like your name, Steve? Steve. Steve. Steve!' Daddy will suddenly say in a loud voice, 'Please don't call me Steve. Just call me "daddy".' Note how the whole shop goes quiet. Daddy will glance around, clocking the pitying looks from fellow shoppers.

A man will approach. He will quietly say to daddy, 'Why not start with "Uncle Steve", mate? It's a lot for the little 'un to take on board, don't you think?'

How mummy will laugh when you tell her what happened.

57 HAVE YOUR TEA IN FRONT OF THE TELLY

Mummy thinks children should eat their meals sitting at a big table with a gingham cloth on it, chatting about their day and listening to classical music. We all know that by the time you're eight you'll be slumped in front of the box like everyone else, glugging Coke and eating peelable cheese. But that time hasn't come yet – mummy's dream is still intact so you'll have to tread carefully.

Start slowly . . . ask for a healthy snack while you're watching *Charlie and Lola*. Mummy will be so pleased that you asked for a bowl of chopped banana, she won't realize what's just happened.

Step by step, day by day, gradually wear her down. Move on from fruit to wholesome foods that produce crumbs (brown toast's ideal). Before you know it you'll be allowed to leave the table and have pudding in front of an educational programme such as *Springwatch*.

And from there it's only a few short steps to the ultimate – American hot pizza while you're watching *EastEnders*. Heaven.

Note: If challenged, point out that this is what mummy does once you've gone to bed.

58 FIND THE 'SWEET SPOT' IN A DOUBLE BED

Moving from the cot to a bed is really fantastic ... because now you're free to spend every night with your parents.

You may be welcomed in at first. If you're not, just wait till they're asleep, then creep in at the end of their bed and scramble up under the covers. Position yourself in the 'sweet spot' – the very middle of the mattress, which, as everyone knows, is the most comfortable part of any bed.

Start off curled up like a little cashew nut, hugging a soft toy to ensure you keep your arms neatly tucked in close to your body. Your parents may wake up now and whisper to each other about how cute you look. Don't engage in any conversation at this point or you're at risk of being sent back to your own bed. Just keep quiet and soon you'll all drift off back to sleep.

Once you get into the REM (rapid eye movement) stage of sleep, feel free to truly relax. Bash mummy in the nose with a flailing arm and kick daddy in the willy as you turn yourself 180 degrees. Sleeping across the bed like this is the most restful part of the entire night, so really enjoy it.

In the morning, nudge mummy (not too hard or she might fall off the edge) and ask her why she's sleeping with her head on the bedside table. Go and look for daddy – he'll be curled up in your toddler's bed. Doesn't he look funny?!

59 SIT AT THE TOP OF A SLIDE AND REFUSE TO BUDGE

The top of a slide is the most powerful position in the entire playground. Not only can you survey everything from this vantage point, but you also have the power to bring all sliding activity to a complete halt for as long as you choose to do so.

Top Tips

* Sit with your legs dangling down the slide. A queue will quickly build up behind you.
* Don't catch the eye of anyone at the bottom – they'll only try to persuade you to come down.
* Don't listen to anyone begging you to get a move on. Just stare ahead and enjoy the power.
* Hold on to the sidebars to prevent other children behind you from pushing you down the slide.
* A bulky coat will fill any gaps at waist level, meaning no one can access the slide to your left or right.

Daddy will try to reach up and grab you – retreat further back to avoid his arms. This will force daddy to come up and get you. Doesn't he look funny crawling on all fours?

The moment daddy gets to you is the perfect time to set off down the slide. Then he will have no option but to come down the slide himself. Let's hope his bottom's not too big!

AGED 2–3 YEARS

30 GET OFF YOUR FACE ON SUGAR

Have you ever noticed how mummy starts laughing hysterically after she's had a glass or two of wine? Or how daddy starts pacing the room challenging people to arm-wrestling competitions after he's had a few 'sharpeners'? Well, their behaviour is down to the effect of a magic liquid known as 'alcohol'. Unfortunately, children aren't allowed to drink 'alcohol' yet, but never fear – something called 'sugar' has exactly the same effect.

Sugar is found in all the yummiest foods – sweets, biscuits, cakes, chocolate and ice cream. However, lots of parents won't let their children eat sugary foods.

Note: the parent who offers you a rice cake as a 'treat' is usually the one who polishes off entire packets of double chocolate chip cookies when you're not looking.

The best way of getting your first taste of the real stuff is to target grown-ups who don't have the same hang-ups as mummy and daddy. Start with the older generation – grandma will probably be only too happy to give you seven chocolate digestives, claiming they're 'very nourishing'. Failing that, zone in on grown-ups who haven't got a clue about kids. Try persuading Auntie Sue, the child-free friend of your parents who's babysitting, that you always have a sherbet Dip Dab and a glass of lemonade before bed. What fun you'll both have playing together till midnight.

AGED 3-4 YEARS

THE TERRIFIC THREES

Good things come in threes – and that includes you!

Now you're three, you're entering the 'Year of the Question'. Like Socrates and Richard Madeley before you, you'll quickly realize that asking a few insightful questions is the best way to learn stuff. On average you should aim to ask thirty-one questions an hour – if you're up for twelve hours then that's 372 questions a day, more if you're what's known as a 'light sleeper'. Obviously, if your parents fail to come up with satisfactory answers, you'll be forced to keep asking them the same question over and over again. Remember, your key word this year is 'why'.

Don't worry about offending anyone – you're too young to know about tact. If you want to know why 'that man' smells, why Auntie Barbara starts crying after she's had a few glasses of wine, or exactly how babies come out of ladies, now's the best time to ask.

Asking questions will gain you knowledge; and knowledge is what separates you from that dreaded group – babies. There's no greater insult to a person of your advanced years than being called 'a baby'. If someone dares to do this, simply lie on the floor and start screaming. That'll show them how grown-up you are.

So, come on all of you, it's time to get started. Altogether now… why-y-y-y-y???

61 GIVE YOURSELF A MAKEOVER

In the early days, your parents probably dressed you up in various silly costumes and had a really good laugh at your expense. Perhaps you've seen the evidence – photographs of yourself dressed as a pumpkin (Halloween), as a bunny (Easter), or with funny glasses and a moustache drawn on with eyeliner (mummy's birthday – she'd had a few drinks). But put those days behind you. It's time you chose your own look.

With some clever tricks and a little know-how, you can easily transform yourself from top to toe. Here are a few simple ideas to inspire you:

* Draw on yourself with indelible marker. The perfect time for doing this is the night before your auntie's wedding, when you're expected to be a flower girl. Don't limit yourself to your body – your face'll look great covered in black squiggles too.

* Customize your existing wardrobe to create something new. Tear your silky party skirt into shreds for that fashionable 'Cinderella' look, or squirt glitter glue over all your T-shirts.

* Spring into summer with a fresh, new look – easily achieved with a pair of safety scissors and that £200 Estée Lauder make-up kit mummy got for Christmas.

Get creative and soon you'll have your own unique style!

62 GET ALL THE UNHEALTHY SNACKS YOU WANT

If your parents are stingy when it comes to snacks, try the following strategies. They'll get the biscuit tin open in no time!

* Use a highly effective phrase such as, 'I just need something to keep me going.' If you're offered something healthy, like grapes, shake your head and explain that you're 'biscuity-hungry'.

* Mummy doesn't like to look mean, so ask her for a snack in front of another grown-up. For example, when the front doorbell goes and mummy's chatting politely to the old lady from across the road. Five minutes earlier she had been saying it's not good to have so much sugar. Now she'll say, 'Go and help yourself, darling.'

* Bamboozle the babysitter. If someone other than your parent is looking after you, carefully explain that mummy and daddy let you have all the treats you want.

* Don't let mummy 'edit' your party bag. You may not know it yet, but before mummy gets hold of them, party bags are full of all sorts of sugary goodness – so it's vital you get to them first. Try asking for a party bag as soon as you arrive, or offer to swap your present with it. Alternatively, spend the entire party hovering round the party-bag table. You won't be able to play any of the games, but it's worth it.

* Help yourself. An essential life skill is to learn how to open the door of the fridge or freezer. However, this does require quite a bit of strength, so you should consider propping it open with a small toy afterwards to save yourself the trouble next time.

63 PARROT THE WORDS TO AN ENTIRE ADVERT

While mummy's trying to show you how to write your name or teaching you to count to ten, why not surprise her with some knowledge you've learnt from the telly?

Say something like: 'Confused about car insurance? Let us quote you today – the price you see is the price you pay. No hidden extras, just give us a call; free personal injury cover, we're there for you all.'

For maximum effect, repeat the advert just as you hear mummy telling her friend how she restricts you to half an hour of telly a day – preferably something educational like *Baby Einstein*. If possible, try to make it an advert about phone lines or plastic surgery. How mummy will laugh.

64 GO HOME IN SOMEONE ELSE'S PANTS

There's a corner of every child's underwear drawer that contains a selection of other children's pants. They will comprise:

* The pants someone lent you when you went visiting without wearing any.

* The pants you borrowed because you wet your own.

* The pants on loan because you stayed for bathtime at somebody else's house.

* The pants you secretly swapped with your friend.

* The pants you put on by accident after a dressing-up session.

Rules for Borrowing Pants

* No mother will give you her child's best pants. She'll give you a tatty pair with an almost-worn-out picture of *Dora the Explorer* or *Fireman Sam* on them.

* A father will give you his child's best pants, because he misguidedly thinks this is what the mother would do.

* If you return the pants, they must have been washed and ironed and be presented in a clear sandwich bag – or not be given back at all.

* Pants that are not handed back may not be lent to other visiting children for at least six months. After that you're safe.

AGED 3-4 YEARS

65 LEARN TO SPIN A DUMMY IN YOUR MOUTH

If you've been lucky enough to hang on to your dummy till now, you don't want to go losing it at this stage. When mummy starts making comments like, 'How about saving it for bed-time?', or even, 'I beg you to give up your dummy – I'll buy you a Nintendo DS', you know you're going to need a new tactic.

Rather than agreeing to give it up on your next birthday, or donating it to 'the poor children', just learn to spin your dummy in your mouth. This clever trick will impress children and adults alike and is always a wow at parties. It'll even help raise your parents' status among their friends again. Here's how you do it:

1. Wander into the room making a loud sucking noise on your dummy, so everyone turns to look at you.

2. Place the tip of your tongue close to the inside of your left cheek.

3. Quickly flick your tongue to the other side of your mouth. This will cause the dummy in your mouth to rotate 180 degrees.

4. Accept the applause.

5. Make a loud sucking noise and wander off.

Simple but effective.

66 MAKE AN UNSUITABLE FRIEND

Why should mummy and daddy always decide who comes over to play? You want someone fun, but they prefer someone 'nice'. Time for you to put your foot down and decide who you want to invite to tea for a change.

Why not start with the Four Unsuitable Friends of the Apocalypse . . . ?

1. **Rude.** He seems quiet and unassuming when he arrives, but Rude soon perks up once his mummy goes. He spends the afternoon vandalizing the house, telling mummy she smells like a poo poo and spitting out any food he doesn't like on to the floor. Rude reverts to his quiet, unassuming behaviour when his mummy returns – she knows better than to ask whether he behaved himself. She'll just pick him up and scarper.

2. **Rash.** Mummy only notices Rash's crop of mystery spots after your friend has tried on the entire contents of your dressing-up box – without her vest on. Mummy makes a mental note to boil-wash everything after Rash has gone. Then her mummy turns up, hangs around drinking endless cups of tea, and suggests you and Rash have a bath together, 'as it's getting late'. Before mummy has the chance to stop her, Rash's mummy has plucked you both out of

the bath and vigorously rubbed you down with the SAME TOWEL. Mummy then spends the rest of the evening scouring the internet for information on 'molluscum' and 'impetigo'.

3. **Naughty.** Naughty seems nice at first. He politely asks if he can pop upstairs to use the bathroom halfway through tea. Mummy watches him disappear, impressed with his beautiful manners. She even says she wishes you were as well behaved as he is. Upstairs, he quickly pours her Origins Ginger Float bubble bath down the sink before putting in the plug, turning the taps on full and then coming back down for pudding.

4. **Scary.** Scary has a scary mummy with a 'cut here' tattoo around her neck and a greying diamanté thong peeking out of her shell-suit bottoms. She's polite enough – stubbing her fag out in the pot of geraniums and putting down her can of extra-strength lager before she comes into the house – so why does mummy check her purse is still there after she's gone?

If mummy complains, just listen to daddy pointing out that she's allowed to have her Unsuitable Friends of the Apocalypse round – Gossipy, Squiffy, Competitive and Bossy. How she'll laugh!

67 WATCH YOUR FAVOURITE FILM FIFTY TIMES

Why would you want to watch something new? You know what you like and you like what you know, and if you've got a favourite film there's no reason to watch any other. After all, it takes thirty viewings to get under the skin of *The Lion King*, forty to understand the subtext of *Beauty and the Beast* and fifty times of watching *Mary Poppins* to learn how to say 'supercalifragilisticexpialidocious'.

In a way, you're just like mummy – she watches *EastEnders* about two hundred times a year, and every episode seems to be the same. Each time she watches it you'll hear the phrases: 'It's my name above the door', 'he's faaaaamily' and 'you're barred'.

Even so, mummy and daddy will try to persuade you to see something else. Perhaps they'll rent *Bambi* from the library, or treat you to a copy of *Shrek*. Ignore them – even though the forty-eighth time they watch *Sleeping Beauty* touching the spindle of the spinning wheel they start to rock backwards and forwards, holding their heads and saying, 'This is doing my nut'. You must stay firm. It's your bedtime routine, your film.

And then one day, for no apparent reason, decide you'd like to watch *High School Musical*. When mummy looks at you in disbelief and asks why you don't want to watch *The Incredibles* as usual, just say, 'I've seen it'.

68 BE GULLIBLE

At your age, it's still hard to tell fact from fiction. You've just got to face it – you're at a time in your life when you probably believe everything mummy and daddy tell you. Do these classic comments ring any bells?

* I didn't bring any money with me. What a shame.
* No, I haven't been eating your chocolate. It must be my chocolate-flavoured toothpaste you can smell.
* Of course I haven't thrown any of your artwork away. It's all filed safely in the loft.
* Never touch my laptop – it's very hot and will burn your fingers.
* This is the very last biscuit in the house.
* There are definitely no vegetables in it.
* I have no idea where the drum set granny gave you for Christmas has gone.
* Never piddle in the swimming pool. They put something in the water that makes it turn purple on contact with wee, so if you do you'll be chucked out.
* What a shame the ice-cream van's playing that tinkly music – it means they've run out of lollies.

They're all lies that mummy and daddy tell you to save money, make their lives easier or just to give themselves a laugh. Get your own back once you've turned five. When mummy tries to get you into Legoland for free by pretending you're still four, loudly ask her why she's lying. She'll be cross at the time, but she'll laugh about it later.

69 SAY SOMETHING SCARY

Mummy and daddy love you very much. You're the apple of their eye. But appear before them on a dark landing, in the middle of the night, wearing a white nightdress, and you'll scare the hell out of them. For one horrific moment you're not their darling daughter, but that little girl from *Poltergeist*.

The initial step is to do something scary. Maybe you've drawn your very first face – two eyes, a mouth, even a squiggle for the nose. Mummy thinks it's so beautiful she wants to frame it – especially when you tell her it's a picture of her. Why not sweetly ask if you can have it back for a moment? Then grab a black pen and get to work . . . scribble over the eyes so hard you make holes in the paper.

Once you've realized the reaction doing something scary creates in your parents, you can move up to the next stage . . . saying something scary. Perhaps you were in the park one time with mummy watching a lovely dog chasing sticks. Maybe mummy told you about 'dog years', and how dogs don't live as long as humans. A few days later, just after mummy's kissed you good night and turned out the lights, you could call out: 'Scooby Doo's going to die before Shaggy.' See the expression on mummy's face!

70 GROW A SUNFLOWER

Some grown-ups make a fuss about gardening, telling you it's really difficult. The truth is, planting stuff is easy – and you can prove it by growing a massive sunflower. Honestly, how tricky can gardening be if a child can grow the biggest and best flower of all, in double-quick time? What you do is:

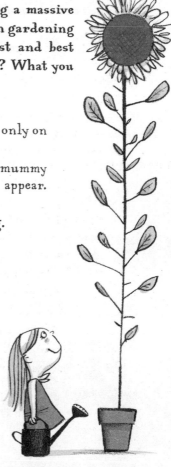

1. Plop a seed into a pot of soil.

2. Water it twelve times a day – but only on the first day.

3. Watch the soil intently, asking mummy when the green bit's going to appear. Wander off, bored.

4. Leave mummy to do the watering.

5. Discover mummy has moved the seedling to a bigger pot. Look at it for a bit, then wander off, bored.

6. Ask a neighbour to water it while you're on holiday. Explain you'll be really upset if it's dead when you come back. She will consider cancelling her weekend away.

7. When the sunflower opens, show it off to everyone. Take all the credit – you deserve it.

71 DIVIDE AND RULE

When it comes to discipline, mummy and daddy try to present a united front. This is bad news when it comes to doing and getting what you want, so you need to learn how to break them down.

The key to success is treating mummy and daddy as two separate units, and working on one parent at a time.

* Carefully log any differences between mummy and daddy in styles of discipline, and then ruthlessly exploit this knowledge. Say things such as: 'But daddy said I could', 'Mummy never makes me eat all my vegetables' and 'You're much nicer than daddy'. (Mummy will tell you off for saying this last one, but secretly she'll love it.)

* Don't be afraid to tell tales. There's a saying in the criminal world that no one likes a grass – in the toddler world this couldn't be more wrong. If you see mummy smoking, or daddy reading the paper when he should be making tea, don't be shy about letting the other parent know. Especially if bedtime is looming. In the ensuing row, you can watch *Space Pirates*.

* You're probably starting to feel the urge to stay in bed later than 5 o'clock in the morning – don't! It's important to keep the pressure up, because one tired parent on their own is easier to exploit than two well-rested parents together. It's the only way to guarantee Coco Pops for breakfast.

72 BURY DADDY IN THE SAND

No day trip to the beach is complete if you haven't covered daddy in sand. Here's what you do:

1. Dig a long, shallow trench in some dry sand – actually, ask daddy to do it.

2. Get daddy to lie down in this hole.

3. Pour sand all over him. Make sure you flick some in his eyes.

4. Leave his head exposed, so he can breathe and is able to drive you home later.

5. Leave one toe out too, so it's available for tickling.

6. Pat the sand down firmly with a spade. How mummy will laugh when you bash him 'in the knackers'.

7. Give him some boobies made out of mounds of sand. Jump up and down saying, 'Daddy's got boobies, daddy's got boobies.'

8. Give him some seaweed hair, and perhaps a mermaid's tail made from sand and shells.

9. Get mummy to take a photograph.

10. Jump on him.

11. Run away screaming as he hauls himself out of the hole like some giant sand monster.

12. Help him look for his car keys, especially if the tide's coming in.

73

DEVISE THE PERFECT CAR JOURNEY

The great thing about being in a car is that you've got a parent on tap, ready to meet all your minute-to-minute needs. It's up to you to make the most of it. The important thing is to make sure you keep those demands coming. Here are some useful things to say during a typical journey:

* Can I have my tapes on? I don't like this one ... can you turn it down? I love this one ... can you turn it up?

* I'm hot ... can you open one of the windows? I'm cold ... can you close one of the windows?

* I'm hungry ... I don't like ham ... uh-oh, I've dropped it. What are you eating? Can I have a biscuit too?

* I want my tapes on! What does Terry Wogan look like?

* I need a wee ... I need it now ... it's coming!

Top tip: *why not get mummy and daddy to invest in a 'Dictator on Board' sticker for the family car?*

As you arrive at your destination feeling relaxed and refreshed, congratulate yourself that your parent – the same one who drove you home from hospital at 3mph all those years ago – has now been trained by you to peel a banana and find a lost shoe while driving at 80mph up the M1. That's really something to be proud of.

74 BECOME THE WORLD EXPERT ON KIDDIE RIDES

Adults never seem to notice children's rides – but you know they're everywhere. Flashing lights, catchy music, maybe a character from your favourite TV show – what's not to like? However, while enjoying kiddie rides is one thing, being an expert is quite another – and the only way to become one is to have a go on them . . . again and again.

Some rides are better than others. Good ones include fire trucks, helicopters, police cars, miniature carousels and ponies. Unknown cartoon characters from Eastern Europe are a definite no-no – unless they're all that's available, in which case they're fantastic.

Note: Some rides are only 20p, some are £1 – it won't be clear why, but it's probably safer to go on the ones for a quid wherever possible.

AGED 3-4 YEARS

75 LEARN A NAUGHTY WORD AND USE IT IN CONVERSATION

Children your age have a great capacity for language, and the best way to add some 'flavour' to your everyday conversation is to introduce a smattering of rude words.

Your parents are the best source of discovering these little gems. Listen out next time daddy's joking with his mate on the phone, or when mummy's shouting at him for leaving his stinky socks by the bed – you're bound to hear some new and exciting words to use, especially if they've no idea you're listening in.

The key to making a rude word 'stick' is to use it in a sentence in general conversation every day for a week. In this way you'll seamlessly and effortlessly integrate naughty words into your vocabulary. For instance, next time granny offers you a slice of cake and asks you what you think of it, smile sweetly and say, 'It's bloody delicious, granny.' Or perhaps on your first visit to a new playgroup you could put your hands over your ears and shout, 'It's a f***ing din in here, mummy. Let's go.'

This is a particularly good trick if you think mummy and daddy are not listening carefully to everything you say – you'll immediately gain their attention, and after this they won't ignore you again.

76 SAY IT LIKE IT IS

Parents say it's important to tell the truth, so feel free to be as honest as you like when you're out and about.

You could loudly enquire, 'Why is that man so fat?' (Extra marks if it's mummy's boss, or a close relative like her father-in-law – that's granddad to you.) Perhaps you could run into an elderly relative's house and say, 'It stinks in here', or ask in her earshot why Mrs Lewis from next door looks like a man. If you're on a bus, why not laugh openly at a stranger's haircut? Or when someone visits your home, ask loudly when they are going to leave. The list is endless.

Make the most of this freedom because, eventually, mummy will point out that you sometimes need to 'bend the truth' a little to spare other people's feelings. Ask her if she's ever done that to you; watch her expression carefully. She'll admit she may have told you the 'odd white lie', though she can't think of any examples right at that moment.

Now's the time to ask if Patch really did run away last week to go and live on a farm. He had been limping really badly, then you were unexpectedly sent to granny's for the afternoon, and you were worried he'd died. Observe mummy's face as she tells you that Patch is absolutely fine ... do you really think she'd lie about a thing like that?

77 HAVE YOUR FIRST THEMED BIRTHDAY PARTY

All you want from a party is a table of sugary foods and a bubble machine. But mummy thinks you should have something similar to her friends' children – that's why she suggests you have a themed party. Why not help her by coming up with a brilliant theme that no one else has ever thought of? At this stage, mummy will become less enthusiastic. She'll suggest you stick to something simple like a princess party or a pirate party, an alien party or an under-the-sea party. Put your foot down – if you can find the relevant partyware in Tesco's, then the theme's not worth bothering with. Explain to mummy that Nigella would always rise to the challenge and make the stuff herself – or at least get her servants to.

So, set your heart on a meerkat party, where everything should match. Time to get those invites out! Here's what mummy will need to prepare:

* A meerkat tablecloth, and meerkat plates and cups.
* Meerkat balloons.
* A meerkat bouncy castle.
* A birthday cake in the shape of a meerkat.
* Sandwiches cut in the shape of meerkats.
* Biscuits cut in the shape of meerkats.

* Hula Hoops, party rings, Jammie Dodgers and mini sausages – no need to bother with the meerkat theme here.
* Meerkat party bags containing meerkat-themed gifts.

All the games must also have a meerkat theme:

* Pin the tail on the meerkat.
* Hunt the meerkat.
* Meerkat says.
* Musical meerkats.
* Pass the meerkat.

If mummy's a WAG, she'll have loads of money and will easily be able to afford a mob of real meerkats to come to your party. If not, an inflatable meerkat will have to do.

As your satisfied guests leave, start planning next year's party. Wouldn't an Aztec theme be nice?

78 MAKE AN IMAGINARY FRIEND

Imaginary friends are better than real ones because you can boss them around and make them do exactly what you want.

Tip: *if mummy and daddy take you to one side and ask you if you're feeling lonely, just smile mysteriously and say, 'Not any more. I've got Izzy-Isabel now.' Then walk away, carrying Izzy-Isabel carefully in the palm of your hand.*

Your imaginary friend is completely invisible to everyone except you – so it's your job to prevent people from treading on them or sitting in their seat at teatime. Perhaps they're a tiny pixie that follows you around, a ferret that nips at your heels or a flying hamster. Perhaps you only see them in your dreams; maybe they're called Mr Beiling and live on the ceiling; or it could be that you can only hear them speak when it's windy. Remember – you make the rules.

Trends come and go – dolphins were incredibly popular twelve months ago, but giants and squirrels are set to be the big hits this year – so get in early before everyone else claims your new friend as their own.

On a final note, if you don't fancy making an imaginary friend, consider making an imaginary enemy instead. They come in very handy if you want someone else to take the blame for any naughtiness you've been up to.

79 CHALLENGE YOUR PARENTS' PRECONCEPTIONS ABOUT GENDER

If you're a boy, why not wear a Disney princess dress to the pirate party daddy organized for your fourth birthday party? Or, if you're a girl, simply refuse to wear that pink dress mummy bought for you, saying 'them clothes are for girls'.

Before they had children, mummy and daddy always swore that any son of theirs would not be allowed to play with toy guns and swords . . . so they'll probably be delighted to see you skipping down the road on the way to your ballet lesson, belting out some fabulous show tunes.

And when it came to having a daughter, mummy went out of her way to buy you a wooden train set and a navy cardigan – it was almost as though she was trying to make a point about something. So she's only got herself to blame now that you insist on running around the garden in camouflage gear and jackboots, hitting people with big sticks.

80 EMBARRASS MUMMY AT THE DOCTOR'S

Mummy's spent years dressing you up in silly outfits, filming you falling over and publicly cleaning your face with a tissue soaked in saliva. Now it's your turn to embarrass her. And the most effective place to do this is at the doctor's, because this is where you can guarantee mummy will be trying to appear her most responsible and grown up.

You might think mummy should know whether you are truly ill or not – after all, you've heard her refer to herself as an 'experienced mother'. But the truth is, mummy hasn't got a clue. Why not show her up in front of a medical professional using your 'pain in the leg' ploy? Here's what you need to do:

1. Get out of bed.
2. Fall over.
3. Limp to the breakfast table saying, 'My leg hurts.'
4. Mummy will then phone the surgery and make an emergency appointment.
5. Watch mummy call work to say she'll be late as her child is desperately ill.

6. One hectic hour later, mummy will carry you into the doctor's consulting room. When the doctor asks you to walk across the room – and this is the crucial bit – you must...

WALK COMPLETELY NORMALLY!

A couple of things will now happen:

* The doctor will look at mummy with an expression that says, 'You're an over-anxious mother, aren't you?'
* Mummy will say sorry to the doctor for wasting their time.

Even though mummy should be relieved you're okay, she will actually look at you as though she wants to kill you.

Other 'medical ailments' to try include:

* The instantly disappearing rash.
* The temperature that suddenly returns to normal.
* The apparently ruptured appendix. Your screaming will convince mummy and daddy this is what's wrong, when in actual fact you've just got your little toe caught sideways in a thread inside your sock.
* The mysterious tummy ache. It should be worrying enough for your parents to cancel their New Year's Eve outing (even though that means they still have to pay the babysitter), but mild enough to disappear completely once you have produced a loud windy pop at ten minutes to midnight.

AGED 4-5 YEARS
THE LAST DAYS OF FREEDOM

You've come a long way, baby, and this is going to be the year you've finally got everything just as you want it. Now, at last, you have all the necessary skills at your fingertips, as well as the confidence to put them into action.

You've got a wonderful imagination which turns your best friend into a pirate and the toilet into a wishing well; a perfectly honed physique that enables you to ride a scooter through a crowded shopping centre at 30mph; and fine motor skills – so accurate you can disable a digital camera in under a minute.

But if there is anything you particularly want to do, then do it now. Jump into that pile of freshly raked leaves, build a den under the dining table, and run around the garden absolutely starkers. Fill your pockets with snails and worms, sprinkle glitter around the house, or see how many times you can jump on a double bed before falling headfirst into the wardrobe. Because this year is your last hurrah: your final opportunity to run riot, have appalling manners and experience total and utter freedom before you go to Big School. Enjoy it while you can.

81 FALL OFF THE BIG SWINGS

You've seen six-year-olds swinging on them, ten-year-olds jumping off them and teenagers smoking on them. Now you've had your fourth birthday, it's your turn on The Big Swings.

Signs you're ready for The Big Swings:

1. You can't get your legs out of The Little Swings.
2. There's a queue at The Little Swings.
3. You're a bit bored.

Ways to fall off The Big Swings:

1. Let go when mummy is pushing, even though she says, 'Don't let go.'
2. Lean forward to look at a stone.
3. Lean backwards to look at the sky.
4. Try to avoid a friend who's come to see what you're doing on The Big Swings.
5. Dodge mummy, who's trying to slow down the swing because she wants to go home.

Note: It doesn't matter which way you decide to fall off The Big Swings – it will always, always be mummy's fault.

82 STOP MUMMY LIVING VICARIOUSLY THROUGH YOU

Mummy's signed you up for ballet, tennis and piano lessons. You don't want to do any of these things – you want to spend your afternoons running in and out of the sprinklers, eating Curly Wurlys and watching telly . . . just like mummy did when she was four.

The thing is, mummy wants YOU to be really brilliant at things so SHE can watch you, show off about you . . . and not bother having to do anything herself. What you need to make mummy realize is, if she's so interested in classical music or formal dance, then perhaps she should be the one signing up.

But how do you get out of going to the lessons? You can't just say you don't want to go any more – you don't want to be accused of 'being a quitter'. And throwing a strop will only make you look ungrateful. Fortunately, there's a very simple strategy to make it all stop . . .

BE RUBBISH AT EVERYTHING!

Mummy's artistic ambitions will soon fade if you repeatedly fail to recognize a single primary colour. And her dreams of an Olympic gold will vanish if you keep the stabilizers on your bike until at least your twelfth birthday.

Once Mummy's readjusted her sights, it's a very short step back to the sprinklers, Curly Wurlys and telly.

83 CLAIM TO HAVE SEEN FATHER CHRISTMAS

Now we all know that Santa exists, but the truth is no one actually ever sees him on Christmas Eve – he just moves too fast. Why not make mummy and daddy's Christmas more exciting by swearing blind you saw him delivering the presents?

It's the details that really matter, so go to town! Tell them you saw his sleigh land on next door's roof, that all the reindeer were there and Rudolph's nose was really glowing. See how confused mummy and daddy look when you explain how Father Christmas sat on top of the chimney to enjoy a couple of mince pies and a glass of sherry. Say that he came to your house next, and you peeked out from under your covers to see him filling the empty pillowcase with presents. Then he asked you if you'd like to help him deliver presents to Norway. Of course you said yes and had a brilliant time! Watch mummy and daddy's faces . . . it's as though they want to say something, isn't it?

Look bright-eyed as you exclaim that even though Santa visited all the boys and girls in the world last night, you're the only one who actually got to ride on his sleigh. You must be the most special child ever, mustn't you?

Stand by your story. Mummy and daddy can't prove you're 'making things up again', can they?

84 TELL YOUR FIRST LIE

It's wrong to lie – but it's a good way to get what you want. It can also get you out of trouble, divert blame or make you look good in front of your friends. Try these:

* I didn't steal it . . . I found it in the park.
* It wasn't me.
* She hit me first.
* I've got a bigger one of those at home.
* The dog ate it.
* My hand just slipped.

If mummy suspects you're fibbing, she'll sit you down and say she'd be crosser with you for lying than she would be if you told her the truth and admitted what you did. Don't fall for that old chestnut – the truth is, you won't get into any trouble at all if you keep schtum.

85 LEAVE THE TOPS OFF YOUR FELT-TIP PENS

Don't waste time putting the lids back on your felt tips after you've done some colouring in – this will take up valuable minutes you can't afford to lose. Unlike an adult, you've only got twelve hours in which to get all the day's chores done – there's *Tom and Jerry* to be watched and cushions to be taken off the sofa – so leaving the tops off your felt tips is an ideal way of making up some extra time.

Now, the persistent felt-tip-pen-top-leaver-offer is bound to encounter some resistance. But do not be swayed. Here are some of the things you are most likely to hear mummy or daddy say:

* **Daddy:** These felt tips are expensive.

   FACT: felt tips have never been cheaper – Asda sells 100 of them for £1.50.

* **Mummy:** When I was little, my felt tips had to last me all year long.

   FACT: this is because she obviously never tried leaving the tops off. Granny or granddad would probably have bought mummy some new ones if she had only showed some backbone.

* **Mummy:** When I was little, felt tips were my main Christmas present.

   FACT: this is true, but if she will write 'felt tips' on her letter to Santa she's only got herself to blame.

86 LEARN TO UNBUCKLE YOUR SEAT BELT IN THE CAR

Question: How do you break the silence on a long, boring car journey?

Answer: Unbuckle your seat belt. That'll get mummy and daddy chatting again.

Nothing will surprise your parents more on the motorway than discovering you can unbuckle your seat belt. Say, 'Look what I've done!' and they'll watch open-mouthed as you clamber down into the well behind the front passenger seat to retrieve that half-sucked lollipop you've had your eye on for months. While you're down there, listen out for phrases such as:

* Pull over now!!!
* There's no hard shoulder!
* I did buckle him in.
* But did you hear it click properly?
* What does that police car want?
* It's my wife's fault, officer.

Note: when you go with daddy to collect mummy from the police station, it's probably wise to agree never to unbuckle your seat belt again.

87 REALIZE SAUSAGES ARE MADE FROM DEAD PIG

You've been to the city farm, you've fed the ducks in the park – you've even started asking for a pet. So it may come as a bit of a shock to discover that those juicy sausages you have for tea are actually made from pigs!

It'll probably take you a while to find out 'The Truth'. When you first ask what sausages are made from, mummy will say, 'Meat ... Now eat up. They're good for you.' One day you'll notice the packaging always has pictures of pigs on it and you'll realize that meat has something to do with animals. When you ask mummy if the animals gave us the sausages, she'll say, 'Sort of ... Now eat up. They're good for you.'

Then comes the day of truth. You have a new friend over for tea. He looks down at the sausages on his plate and says, 'I don't eat dead animals. I'm a vegetarian.' You pause for a minute. You then turn to mummy and ask her, 'Have we been eating dead animals?' Watch her hesitate before smiling sweetly and saying, 'Yes, darling, but we only eat animals that have had a good life.' And note the way she sneaks the 'bargain bangers' packet into the bin before your friend's mummy arrives.

Perhaps mummy will worry about how you'll react next time you visit the farm. Put her mind at rest by running over to the pigsty, leaning in and saying, 'Hey, I'm going to eat you soon.' Mummy will be so relieved.

88 THROW A TANTRUM AT LEGOLAND

It may be a while since you had a full-blown tantrum – perhaps even a couple of years. But remember, the best are always the ones your parents didn't see coming – who'd have thought you'd go ballistic on a lovely day out at a theme park! So here's how it goes:

1. After daddy has handed over a week's wages, you can visit the theme park and have a fantastic time.

2. Go on all the rides and eat sweets till you feel sick.

3. When mummy says this is the last ride of the day, start whining.

4. Go on ride.

5. Hang on to mummy's leg, begging for one more go.

6. Go on ride again.

7. Ask for one final go. This time mummy will refuse.

8. Throw yourself on the floor. Start to scream.

9. Go completely floppy, so mummy can't pick you up.

10. Go completely rigid like a plank. Daddy won't be able to get you into the buggy designed for a 'sitting' child.

11. Keep crying till you're totally exhausted.

12. Let mummy or daddy carry you to the car. Fall asleep on the way.

13. Once the tantrum's over, it's over. Forget it ever happened.

AGED 4-5 YEARS

89 BELIEVE TOYS ARE REAL

As proven in the investigative documentary *Toy Story*, and its excellent follow-up *Toy Story 2*, toys are real. If people don't believe you when you tell them so, here's the proof:

* You always find your toys neatly lined up on the shelf when you get home from nursery, even though you left them on the floor as you set off that morning.

* Teddy is always hard to find at bedtime. It's not because you've forgotten where you left him – it's because he's gone off for a stroll before turning in for the night.

* If you don't play with your toys for a while they'll run away – to somewhere like a local charity shop or car boot sale (see notes below on how to prevent them from doing this).

* Toys come to life when you're out or asleep. That's why they always stay very still when you're around – they're absolutely exhausted.

Note: demonstrate that you play with every-thing the whole time by spreading all your toys across the bedroom floor every day. Scribble on them with indelible marker pen to make it easier for people to know they belong to you, so they will then return the toys to you if they abscond.

AGED 4-5 YEARS

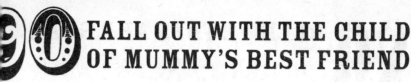

FALL OUT WITH THE CHILD OF MUMMY'S BEST FRIEND

Mummy's finally crawling back up the social ladder and has made a friend: one she really likes – not just someone to chat to about the pros and cons of the MMR vaccine.

The trouble is you don't like her kid. Nothing's actually wrong with them, but you just don't 'click'. Although tempted to go on a play date, so both mummies can chat, just stop and think. Do you really want to spend your holidays with this child? Or hang out with them when you're seven? If the answer's 'no', now is the time to cut the cord of friendship. It seems ruthless but it's kinder in the long run.

This process will take time. Start small. Hang around mummy instead of playing with your 'friend'. Climb on to mummy's lap. She'll try to push you away, saying you're making her spill her coffee, but refuse to leave. Both mothers will say that perhaps you're tired, or coming down with something. They'll make any excuse rather than voice their biggest fear – their kids don't like each other.

Then take it up a level. Refuse to share any of your toys. Perhaps hint that the other child hit you. Finally, start faking nightmares before each play date, to show mummy how upset you're feeling. Eventually, mummy will have to end her friendship. Of course she'll be upset, but don't worry – she'll have more time to spend with you now.

91 PUT ON A SHOW (EVEN IF YOU DON'T HAVE A SHOW)

You want fame? Well, fame costs. And right here is where you start paying . . . by putting on a show in your bedroom. Well, even Dame Judi Dench had to start somewhere.

Announce to the grown-ups that 'the show will begin in ten minutes'. Go upstairs and get ready. Then you:

1. Dress up – put on scarves, strings of beads and mummy's shoes.
2. Make tickets.
3. Switch off the lights and close the curtains.
4. Set out chairs or cushions for adults to sit on.
5. Arrange teddies and dolls on the chairs and cushions.

AGED 4-5 YEARS

When your audience arrives, you need to:

1. Hand out the tickets.
2. Ask for the tickets back.
3. Show your audience to their seats.
4. Explain that teddies and dolls need the seats so grown-ups will have to sit on the floor.

Run on to the 'stage' and announce: 'Ladies and gentlemen. Welcome to the show.' They will applaud. Run off, giggling. Now:

1. Return to the stage.
2. Stand there for a moment trying to remember what happens first in the show.
3. Remember you didn't actually write a show.
4. Busk it.
5. Jump up and down, shouting and screaming. Maybe leap on to a bed or sofa. Keep the noise levels up to fill in any embarrassing gaps.
6. After a few minutes, the grown-ups will ask you 'to sing a song for the finale'. Tell them firmly that the 'show's not finished yet'. Carry on shouting.
7. When the adults get up to go, tell them there will now be an interval and you'll call them back later.
8. Unfortunately, you may find it difficult to persuade your audience to return. It's their loss . . . what do they know about art?

92 DEVELOP A PHOBIA

By having a phobia you are showing you're not an everyday, run-of-the-mill child, but a more complex and interesting person. Consider starting with a classic childhood fear – the dark, loud noises, thunder or spiders.

Note: Equally disturbing to a grown-up is a child who collects spiders and keeps them in boxes, especially if you start calling yourself King or Queen of the Spiders.

Other classics include a fear of clowns, a firm belief there's a monster living under your bed or that a big hand is going to come up the loo while you're sitting on it and drag you down into the drains. From this, you might want to move on to more unusual phobias, fearing such things as people who wear glasses, pictures of Jesus or the idea your dressing gown is going to get down from the back of your door in the middle of the night and start walking towards you.

93 NEVER LEAVE A MUSEUM EMPTY-HANDED

The only way out of a Las Vegas hotel is through the gaming halls, and the only way out of a museum or gallery is through the gift shop. It is your duty to buy something. If mummy complains, remind her it's her fault for bringing you to see a Rothko retrospective – the least she can do is buy you the commemorative rubber.

Why Parents Take You to Museums

* To expose you to art.
* To impress their friends that they're exposing you to art.
* To convince themselves their lives haven't changed since they had children.
* It's free. Or cheaper than Legoland.
* It's inside. Handy if it's raining.

Since museums have had to compete 'in the marketplace', the range of goods in their shops has improved dramatically. For instance, the British Museum's guide book has recently been replaced by the complete range of Bratz products.

Shopping Strategies

* Aim high. Beg effectively and you might get a talking robot, a cuddly toy or a space hopper. However, bear in mind that you are more likely to emerge with a bouncy ball, a plastic dinosaur or a mug with your name on it.
* Any gift without an educational slant is perfect and should be accepted graciously. But if your parents insist 'it's an educational toy or nothing', then you'll have no option but to go with it. Just chuck it under your bed when you get home and forget about it.
* Never, ever be palmed off with a postcard. These are rubbish.
* A pot of National Trust jam is not a suitable gift for a child.

94 PULL A PLASTER OFF IN ONE GO

Having a plaster put on is fun – especially if it has one of your favourite cartoon characters on it. However, having the plaster pulled off your skin a day later is much more painful . . . but it's something you've got to do.

The Scenario

1. You'll say you don't want to take the plaster off.
2. Mummy says the air needs to get to your skin.
3. You'll persuade her to let it soak off in the bath.
4. After two hours the plaster will still be intact.
5. Daddy will say it has to be ripped off.

Daddies are split into two categories when it comes to this:

* **Those who pull a plaster off slowly.** This means the pain is less but it goes on for much, much longer.
* **Those who pull a plaster off quickly.** There is a lot of pain, but it is over very fast.

It very much depends on your father's occupation as to which camp he falls into. Tax inspectors, vicars and plumbers are more likely to go for the first option, because they like to solve problems one tiny step at a time. Policemen, salesmen and PE teachers prefer the second approach, because they like to get results using the short, sharp shock method.

Note: If daddy's a doctor, you won't have been given a plaster in the first place.

GET THE 'IT' SHOES

95

Owning the 'hot' shoe of the season is sure to impress everyone on your first day at school, so you'd better get them now. It doesn't matter whether they fit properly or how much cash mummy has to spend – as long as they're the ones that everyone else wants, you'll have made a great choice. The hottest store trends:

* Dinosaur holograms – super scary!
* Flashing heels – the more you stamp, the more they flash.
* Wheels in the sole – great for pavement-cruising.
* Laces with bells on – your future teacher will love the tinkling sound, especially if everyone else in the class gets a pair too.

Don't be seen dead in:

* A T-bar sandal.
* Anything in black, brown or navy.
* Anything with Velcro straps – what's wrong with lace-ups for four-year-olds?
* A black plimsoll.
* Anything that mummy likes.

96 POST YOUR LETTER TO FATHER CHRISTMAS BEFORE MUMMY HAS SEEN IT

Get your letter off to Santa early – he's a busy man. It doesn't matter if it's not proper writing. He will still be able to read it. Mummy may seem a bit irritated that you've done this without consulting her. She will also become very interested in what you wrote in your letter – but don't tell her.

Note to mummy: tampering with the Royal Mail is actually an offence.

Mummy will say things like:

* 'What did you ask Father Christmas for?'
* 'I'm seeing Santa's elves later. Why don't you tell me what you want and I'll let them know?'
* 'Will you give me a clue?'
* Or simply – 'Please tell me what you want for Christmas?!'

To all of the above, there is only one answer – 'Santa knows.'

97 GO TO THE PUB

Mummy and daddy love going to the pub. Sometimes, when they're desperate to go and they can't get a babysitter, they'll take you along 'as a treat'.

First, mummy will take you aside and explain this is a one-off and that you'd better be good. She'll tell you how lucky you are to be allowed in through the pub's hallowed doors, because when she was little she had to wait outside in the car with only a packet of smoky-bacon crisps for company. The truth is the law has changed since then and mummy would be arrested if she left you in a pub car park all night.

Whatever you do, don't bother with the beer garden, especially if it contains climbing frames – these are a pub landlord's cynical ploy to keep children outside and away from all the action. You need to be inside the pub, where healthy drinks such as Coca-Cola and lemonade come out of a hose and there are greasy snacks everywhere – it's like Willy Wonka's chocolate factory, but with crisps.

Once inside, there are loads of things you can do:

* Run up to old men and ask them what that horrible brown stuff is that they're drinking.
* Stop couples canoodling by saying, 'Yuk, disgusting'.
* Walk in front of a darts board in the middle of a game.
* Help yourself to those brightly coloured balls on the pool table.
* Press one of the flashing buttons on the fruit machine – but best to run away when the red-faced man shouts, 'Hey, I still had three nudges!'

At first mummy will try to stop you from doing these things. But after she's had a couple of drinks she'll relax and ignore any comments from the 'regulars'.

98 TELL YOUR BABYSITTER ALL THE FAMILY SECRETS

Next time mummy and daddy go out, why not sit up all night with the babysitter? She'll be fascinated by what your family gets up to behind closed doors — especially if she's a close friend or relative — and you'll get to share her crisps. Entertain her with the following secrets:

* Daddy does windy pops when he's in bed.

* Mummy likes to lie on the sofa watching daytime telly and eating Pringles.

* Mummy is always home when you ring — she just tells me not to pick up because you've got 'verbal diarrhoea'.

* Mummy and daddy are thinking about emigrating soon, but don't want you to know. (This is a good one to tell granny if she's babysitting.)

* Daddy's lost his job and has to hide upstairs if anyone comes to visit during the day.

* Mummy has never washed the sheets on your bed. Never ever.

* Mummy and daddy hate that ornament you gave them. They keep it in the shed and only bring it out when you're coming round.

* Daddy thinks I'm much cleverer than your children.

* Mummy thinks you dye your hair too dark.

* Mummy says it's a shame you married Uncle Derek — you could've done much better for yourself. What does 'do much better for yourself' mean?

AGED 4–5 YEARS

99 DEVELOP A SUPERPOWER

Toys are fun and telly's great, but don't be bound by the laws of physics when looking for ways to enjoy yourself. Why not develop a superpower? Something like telepathy, being able to breathe underwater, or the ability to travel back and forth in time. If you believe your superpowers are real, then they are real.

* Close your eyes. You can't see anyone, which means no one can see you. There-fore, you are invisible.

* If you are able to fly, it's probably best done at night when everyone's asleep, so you don't make all the other kids jealous.

* Mummy always comments on how loudly you shout when you want something from her. Explain to her it's because you've got a sonic scream, which enables you to generate much higher amplitude of vocal sound waves than a regular human being.

Unfortunately, these superpowers will eventually fade. Superman had kryptonite to bring him down – and soon you'll have older kids at school telling you that you don't have any powers at all. So make the most of it now while you're still four years old.

100 CATCH DADDY MAKING A HOLLOW THREAT

Daddy says it's bad to lie, but sometimes he does it himself in the form of the 'hollow threat'. This is where he will promise to punish you terribly unless you do exactly what he says – even though he has no intention of carrying this out.

Here are some examples of common hollow threats you might recognize:

* **Hollow Threat One:** 'If you don't finish your breakfast now we won't go on holiday.'

   The Truth: Daddy has already spent a lot of money on the holiday, he's booked the time off work and you're definitely leaving in half an hour – breakfast or no breakfast.

* **Hollow Threat Two:** 'If you don't tidy your room now, I'm calling Max's mummy and telling her you won't be coming to tea later on.'

   The Truth: Daddy's already arranged to play golf, his mate's picking him up later, and you're going to Max's whether you room's tidy or not.

* **Hollow Threat Three:** 'If you don't do that now, I'm calling the police.'

The Truth: Of course, there's no way he's going to call the police. Going to bed without brushing your teeth is not a crime, and daddy would be arrested for wasting police time.

In short, the following should happen if he makes any of these threats:

1. You say, 'Go on, then.'
2. He says, 'Okay, I will.' Perhaps he'll even reach for the phone.
3. A standoff will develop.
4. Keep your cool; do not blink first.
5. Daddy will give you the chance to change your mind.
6. Stay put.
7. Daddy will eventually break and say something like, 'You're impossible. Get in the car, then.'

Note: Look at daddy's face carefully – he always goes a bit red when you catch him telling porkies, doesn't he?

101

HAVE YOUR FIRST DAY AT SCHOOL

There's been a buildup for weeks. Your hair has been cut, your shoes are polished. This can only mean one thing – your first day at school.

Mummy gives you a kiss. Daddy pats your head and says he's proud of you. Granddad mutters something about how you won't experience real freedom again till the day you retire. You walk nervously up the school driveway. Your teacher shows you where to hang your coat and which drawer is yours. After a few moments, mummy and daddy are asked to leave. They smile bravely and walk out, fighting back the tears.

You get through the day just fine. There's a story, and a tray of sand to play with; you do some dressing up and run around outside. It's not too bad at all. In fact you start to wonder why everyone's been making such a fuss.

You come home happy at the end of the day, pleased that such a momentous occasion has passed without incident and that you can get back to your normal life. Then you notice mummy packing your lunchbox and laying out another polo shirt. You turn to her, confused, and ask, 'What? I've got to go back again tomorrow?'

AGED 4–5 YEARS